Listener's Handbook

*A guide to
music
appreciation*

A guide to music appreciation

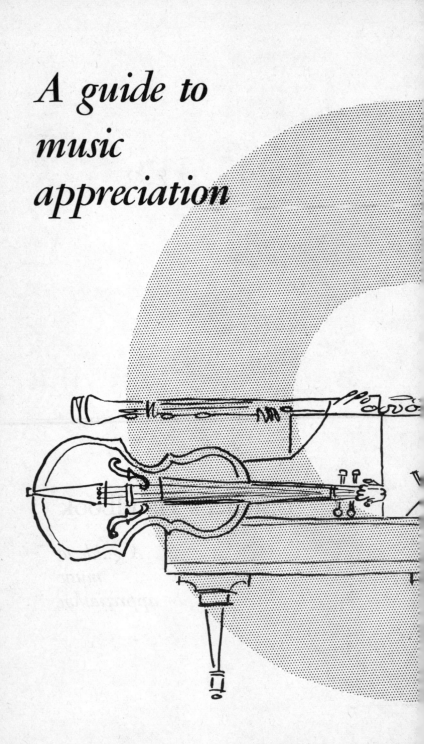

Listener's Handbook

IRA SCHROEDER

Associate Professor
Department of Music
Iowa State University

Iowa State University Press
Ames, Iowa, U.S.A.

IRA SCHROEDER, associate professor of music at Iowa State University, is a world-renowned carillonneur. He has taught classes in music appreciation since 1949, as well as teaching piano. In 1960 he was elected Musical Advisor for the Guild of Carillonneurs in North America and is responsible for editing and publishing carillon music for the Guild. He has traveled extensively throughout the United States, Canada, and Europe appearing as guest carillonneur as well as being university carillonneur at Iowa State. The author received his B.Mus. degree from Bush Conservatory of Music, Chicago, in 1927. He came to Iowa State University in 1931 after teaching for four years at Bush.

First edition 1958

Second edition 1962
Second printing 1963

Library of Congress Catalog Card Number: 62–19767

Preface

This book is written for listeners who know very little or nothing about the various kinds of music literature. Anyone can learn to understand and enjoy listening to music if he wants to. We all have the ability and can develop the capacity to appreciate the best in music even though we may not know one note from another or have any knowledge about the technical side of either composing or performing. The listener is the third party. Listening to and understanding music takes time and effort but the reward is well worth while.

At no time in history have we had so great an opportunity to hear the best of music performed by the finest artists. This is made possible through radio, television and recordings. The most important of all of these is the last. We all enjoy music that we are acquainted with, and what better way can we find to get acquainted with music than by having a record that we may hear over and over when we want to.

There comes a time when we have heard our favorite piece enough and we want to branch out into new fields. These exploratory journeys can become extremely interesting and fascinating because there is literally endless variety.

This book is organized to assist the beginner — to help him get started in an organized way to find his way around in the various periods and trends of musical development, to help him find the different kinds of music that may interest him, to help him organize and set up his own library of recorded music and, best of all, to show him avenues of exploration.

The technical terms are explained in ordinary language and the reader is given tips on how to listen to various kinds of music and what to expect of the music itself. There is music for every mood and occasion.

In the space arts we often find examples of paintings, buildings or sculpturing that are considered mediocre or poor artistically. For economic reasons, many buildings of poor design survive for many years, even centuries, but in music we do not need to be concerned about what is good or bad because only worthwhile music has survived. In this the beginner must trust. According to estimates, about 90 per cent of all music written as serious music fails to stand the test of time.

The suggestions listed in each category are among the more interesting or appealing in that particular classification

So often we hear someone way, "I know what I like." What he is really saying is that he likes what he knows. If you are cooperative, receptive, attentive listener, you will have endle hours of pleasure in exploring the field of music. Listening t music is a very satisfying hobby that can be shared with many It is one of the arts that makes up the most important art of all — the art of living.

Ira Schroeder

6

Contents

8

1

The Elements of Music

Music has seven elements. They are: (1) rhythm, (2) melody, (3) harmony, (4) tempo, (5) dynamics, (6) form and (7) color. Sometimes one or more of these elements are more important or predominant than others.

(1) Rhythm, for all practical purposes, is regular recurring accents. It is sometimes referred to as "meter." Except in irregular rhythms, often found in twentieth-century music, accents divide the beats into groups of twos or threes, or multiples of these. For example, the waltz has an accent on the first beat of each group of three beats — ONE, two, three — ONE, two, three — etc. A march usually has a strong accent on the first beat of each group of four and a lesser accent on the third beat — ONE, two, Three, four — ONE, two, Three, four — etc.

(2) A melody may be very simply defined as a "tune." It may be very evident or a little obscure. Melodies or melodic lines may or may not be singable. So often someone complains about music — especially some twentieth-century music — saying, "It has no tune." Melodies of different periods, different trends and different composers vary in type and degree of importance. All music has melody, but sometimes the rhythm or some other element is more important.

(3) Harmony is the chordal structure or a combination of tones that are sounded simultaneously. These combinations may sound happy, sad, plaintive or any number of describable or indescribable ways. There are those chords or combinations of tones that are dissonant. These serve a definite

11

purpose. They create vigor and give the music added character and contrast.

Paintings are not all sweet, depicting the beautiful. Think of the number of masterpieces of the Crucifixion — the saints being burned at the stake! Sweet lullaby music would certainly be out of place as a counterpart to these.

(4) Tempo is the speed at which a composition is taken. A funeral march has an entirely different effect than a military march. Tempo is a very important element of expression in all of the time arts such as music, drama, ballet, movies, radio and television. In a drama, tempo is very important because different moods require different speeds. For example, it would be just as ridiculous to have slow conversation about an exciting football game as it would be to have fast conversation at the bedside of a dying friend. In music, tempo is just as important in portraying various moods.

(5) Dynamics in music means volume. This is a very important element of expression, relating directly to the mood or drama of the music. A ballet of sylphs might be accompanied very softly by a harp but a rough and ready gypsy dance would require a much louder and more rugged type of music.

(6) Form is the design or the structure of music. All music has some sort of structure varying from a strict form to a very free form. By strict form we mean music that conforms to definite patterns such as rondo, ternary form and sonata form (see Glossary). By free form we mean a composition that is developed with unity and a feeling of balance without holding to patterns. Strict and free form may be likened to formal and informal gardens. The formal garden has definite design while the informal has a more "natural" appearance, yet the informal has a "feeling" of organization.

(7) Color in music is the psychological interpretation of the quality of sound produced by any instrument(s), voice(s), device(s) or any combination thereof. We think of bright or dark colors in connection with the timbre or tone color of the different orchestral instruments, combinations of instruments human voices and the changes of the human voice that occur under different emotional circumstances. The top range of the brilliant trumpet, for example, is much brighter in color than the low tones of the tuba.

2

Instruments of the Symphony Orchestra

ORGANIZATION AND SEATING PLAN OF THE CONVENTIONAL SYMPHONY ORCHESTRA

The instruments of the orchestra are divided into four choirs. They are the string, wood-wind, brass and percussion choirs. Symphony orchestras differ greatly in seating plans and number of individual instruments. The following is an outline of the instruments in their various choirs.

I. Stringed Instruments (String Choir)
    Violins
    Violas
    Violoncellos ('Cellos)
    Double Basses
    Harp
    Harpsichord
    Piano (sometimes classified as percussion)

II. Wood-Wind Instruments (Wood-Wind Choir)
    Piccolo (no reed)
    Flutes (no reed)
    Clarinets (one reed)
    Saxophones (one reed)
    Oboes (two reeds)
    English horns (two reeds)
    Bassoons (two reeds)
    Contrabassoons (two reeds)

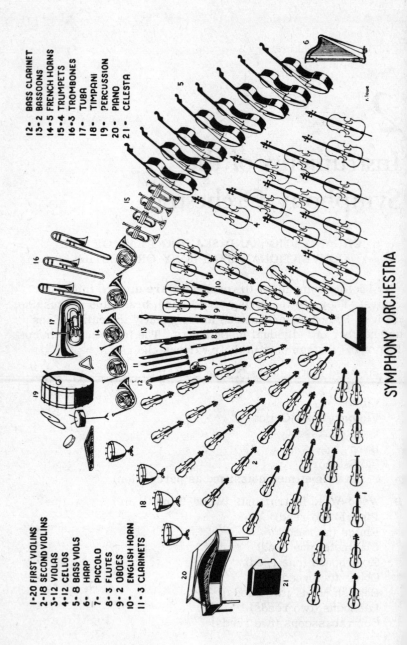

1-20 FIRST VIOLINS
2-18 SECOND VIOLINS
3-12 VIOLAS
4-12 CELLOS
5-8 BASS VIOLS
6- HARP
7- PICCOLO
8-3 FLUTES
9-2 OBOES
10- ENGLISH HORN
11-3 CLARINETS

12-2 BASS CLARINET
13-2 BASSOONS
14-5 FRENCH HORNS
15-4 TRUMPETS
16-3 TROMBONES
17- TUBA
18- TIMPANI
19- PERCUSSION
20- PIANO
21- CELESTA

SYMPHONY ORCHESTRA

r. lowe

14

III. Brass Instruments (Brass Choir)
    Trumpets
    Cornets (seldom used any more)
    French Horns
    Trombones
    Tubas

IV. Percussion Instruments (Percussion Choir)

Timpani (Kettle-Drums)	Glokenspiel
Bass Drum	Xylophone
Side Drum	Castanets
Snare Drum	Tambourine
Chimes	Celesta
Cymbals	Marimba
Gong	Vibraphone
Triangle	Etc., etc.,

DESCRIPTION OF THE INSTRUMENTS

There are a few general ideas that apply to all of the instruments of the orchestra. The smaller they are, the higher the pitch; the larger they are, the lower the pitch. Compare the violin in size with his big brother the double-bass, the piccolo with the flute or the trumpet with the tuba. In the string choir the instruments having the longest strings sound the lowest. Likewise the wind instruments having the longest air column have the lowest pitches.

The thinner the air column, the more brilliant the tone color. Compare the bass trombone with the tuba. They may both sound the same pitch but the trombone will have a much more brilliant and penetrating quality. In other words, the "fatter" the instrument, the more smooth and mellow the tone will be. The bass clarinet looks a great deal like a saxophone except that the saxophone is much "fatter" and consequently sounds much more mellow. The saxophone is much more valuable in a band than in an orchestra because its mellowness aids in blending the more brilliant instruments.

It is rather easy to learn to identify the flute by its sound because it is like a smooth-sounding whistle. Its little brother, the piccolo, is like a very shrill, high whistle. In the flute family we have what may be called the soprano, alto and bass.

15

These instruments have no reeds — the tone is rather open and clear.

Reeds serve as vibrators for the air columns in the one-reed and two-reed instruments. The tone color of these instruments is referred to as "reedy." The one-reed instruments are the clarinet and the saxophone. The saxophone has a much more mellow quality as explained above. The clarinet family has a soprano, alto and double-bass (sometimes called bass clarinet, pedal clarinet or contrabass clarinet). The saxophone family is made up of the sopranino (high soprano), soprano, alto, tenor, baritone and bass.

The two-reed instruments, the oboe, English horn, bassoon and contrabassoon, are rather nasal sounding. This quality of tone color is created by the reeds vibrating against each other. The oboe has the most brilliant and penetrating sound. The English horn is much larger than the oboe and has a more mellow tone quality. It has a pear-shaped end. The oboe has a thinner air column than the English horn. The bassoon has about the same tone quality as the oboe but it seems to be a little more mellow sounding because it is pitched much lower. It has a very long tubelike air column which is wrapped around and around, hence the European name for the instrument, fagotto (bundle of sticks). The contrabassoon sounds an octave lower than the bassoon. These two instruments are often called the clowns of the orchestra.

The trumpet and cornet may well be called the soprano of the brass choir. They are the smallest of this group and play the same pitches. The trumpet is more brilliant because it has thinner tubing than the cornet and because of the brilliance, is more popular.

The trombone because of its thinness is also brilliant. It has a family of four: tenor, bass, tenor-bass and double-bass. The trombone is actually a bass trumpet.

The French horn is easily recognized because it is the most mellow of the smaller horns. Its tubing is wound around in almost a perfect circle.

The tuba, the largest of all the brass choir, is very "fat." It plays the mellow bass parts, has various shapes for various purposes. The name "tuba" is quite loosely used in connection with any bass horn. There are various ranges so that some are called tenor tuba, bass tuba, double-bass tuba and the

Wagner tuba. The musician has much more facility on the last than on any other bass horn.

We suggest that the listener become familiar with the timbre of the highest sounding and lowest sounding instruments first. After that the middle ranged instruments will be easier to identify.

The percussion choir is made up of instruments that produce sound when struck. The drums are timapni (kettle-drums), bass drum, side and snare drums. The side and snare drums are the same except the snare drum has snares or wires stretched across one head and is beaten on the other. The side drum has no snares. Everyone is acquainted with the bass drum — the largest and lowest in pitch. The timpani or kettle-drums are shaped like half of a ball and are tuned to different pitches.

Other percussion instruments are chimes, cymbals (large metal discs), gong (huge suspended metal disc which is struck by a bass drum stick), triangle, glockenspiel or bell lyre (metal bars on a frame shaped like a lyre), castanets, tambourine, celesta (bell-like sounding instrument played from a keyboard like a piano), xylophone (keys of hard wood), marimba (similar to the xylophone but has metal resonating tubes placed beneath the wooden keys), vibraphone (similar to the marimba but has electrically operated vibrators), wind machine (a machine that makes a sound like wind), and all sorts of instruments for sound effects like wood-blocks, sand-blocks, and various noise-making devices.

IDENTIFYING INSTRUMENTS
BY THEIR TIMBRE

The "Nutcracker Suite" by Tchaikovsky is an excellent orchestral suite through which to acquaint yourself with the timbre or tone color of the different instruments. It is well to listen for one instrument at a time. The outline given below mentions various instruments where they have important parts.

There are two forms mentioned (see the Glossary for Rondo form and Ternary form). As you get better acquainted with this suite you will recognize the ternary form in other places than those mentioned. The ones that are mentioned are easiest to recognize. The same is true of the instruments

— you will soon recognize instruments other than those under-
scored in the outline.

"The Nutcracker Suite," Peter Tchaikovsky, Op. 71 a.

1. "Miniature Overture" — Rondo form A-B-A-C-A-B-A-C.
   The "A" melody is played first by the strings, the "B"
   melody by the flute and the "C" melody by the strings.
   Listen for the tinkling triangle in "A."

2. "March" — Listen for two short tunes, one by the horns, the
   other by the strings, punctuated by the cymbals. Note that
   another in the middle section is played by the flutes.

3. "Dance of the Sugar-Plum Fairy" — The celesta plays the
   most important part. At the very beginning it seems to
   be having a little conversation with the bass clarinet.

4. "Trepak" — This is with full orchestra. Note the tambourin

5. "Arab Dance" — This is an excellent composition with which
   to learn to identify the members of the wood-wind choir.
   At various times the different members of this choir take
   the melody. All strings are muted. A mute is a clasp tha
   is placed on the bridge of a stringed instrument to give it
   a quiet, sombre and sort of mysterious effect. The melodies are played by the instruments in this order: clarinet
   muted violins, bassoon, muted violins, clarinet, oboe, Eng
   lish horn, clarinet. Note that near the end we hear the
   clarinet, oboe and English horn each in his turn playing
   the melody one right after the other.

6. "Chinese Dance" — The first instruments that you will hear
   are the bassoons, playing staccato (very short notes). Th
   stringed instruments are played by plucking the strings
   with the fingers. This is called pizzicato. The flute has
   the first melody, a short tune which it repeats immediatel
   Then the piccolo joins the flute playing the same sort of
   tune turned upside down. This is called inversion.

7. "Dance of the Toy Flutes" — This is in ternary form
   (A-B-A). (A) Three flutes, a little extra melody by the
   English horn — (B) Brass choir, melody by trumpets.
   Listen for the rhythmic pattern played by the timpani.

18

8. "Waltz of the Flowers" — Introduction by the wood winds and French horn, harp cadenza (a part played by a solo instrument, usually with considerable technical display), short melody by French horns, alternating with short melody by clarinet, strings alternate with wood-wind choir etc. From here on, try to identify as many instruments as you can.

3

Pre-Renaissance

(600-1400)

Music of the Pre-Renaissance is practically all vocal-monophonic or polyphonic. A single unaccompanied melody is called monophonic. Polyphonic music has two or more melodies played or sung simultaneously. The term "polyphonic" refers preferably to early music.

The Gregorian Chant is the most important music of this period. Although madrigals and motets came into being at this time, the earliest ones of interest to the average listener will be found among those written during the Renaissance.

The Gregorian Chant is a monophonic, liturgical chant of the Roman Catholic Church, named after Pope Gregory (590-604), who collected and standardized their use in the church services. The Gregorian Chant, traditionally unaccompanied, has no set rhythm but is more or less oratorical, conforming to the meaning of the text. It is "syllabic" when there is one note to a syllable and "melismatic" when there are two or more notes to a syllable. There are also times when there is recitation on a single tone.

The chants that were added to the Gregorian collection gradually changed and during the 13th century became known as plainsongs. Most plainsongs have accompaniments and are rhythmically free somewhat like the chants. The terms "chant" and "plainsong" have become synonyms in their general usage.

Those brought up in the traditions of the church are able to sing the chants in authentic style, since much of the interpretation that cannot be written has passed down from generation to generation within the church. For this reason, it is desirable to choose recordings sung by monk's and boy's choirs, trained in the church.

The chants are a devout and sincerely impressive part of the service and tend to deepen the religious experience. They are a part of the Mass, which is a commemoration of Christ's sacrifice on the cross, and are parts of the Proper and the Ordinary of the Mass (see Renaissance).

Suggested Gregorian Chants:

        Miscellaneous Chants by the Benedictine Monks

        Christmas Vespers

        Easter Sunday Mass

        Ordinary of the Mass

4

Renaissance

(1400-1600)

Music of the Renaissance may be characterized as being predominantly polyphonic. During this period composers developed what may be termed, according to present day standards, rational methods of writing. The average listener will enjoy the choral music most of all — the motet, madrigal and Mass.

A motet of the Renaissance period may be defined as a polyphonic choral composition with a sacred text. It is usually designed to be sung in a sacred service and most often it is unaccompanied. There are of course a few exceptions. Some motets are for solo voice, some have secular texts, etc., but the above definition may be used as a general guide and is certainly not confusing to the average listener.

A madrigal of the Renaissance period may generally be defined as a polyphonic unaccompanied choral composition with a secular text — usually pastoral or contemplative in character. The use of the term "madrigal" underwent many changes but the foregoing definition may be used as a general guide for the madrigal of this period, especially the latter part of the Renaissance.

The Ordinary is the part of the Mass that remains constant throughout the church year or calendar. It contains the Kyrie, Gloria, Credo, Sanctus and Agnus Dei — the parts of the Mass that are most frequently sung in the polyphonic Mass. The Benedictus and the Hosanna in Excelsis, often sung, follow the Sanctus.

The Proper of the Mass is that portion which changes with

the church calendar — Advent, Christmas, Epiphany, Lent, Palm Sunday, Easter, etc.

The Ordinary of the Mass may be translated as follows:

KYRIE

Lord, have mercy upon us.
Christ, have mercy upon us.
Lord, have mercy upon us.

GLORIA

Glory be to God on High, and on earth peace, good will
    towards men.
We praise thee, we bless thee, we worship thee, we glorify
    thee,
We give thanks to thee for thy great glory,
O Lord God, heavenly King, God the Father Almighty.
O Lord, the only begotten Son, Jesus Christ;
O Lord God, Lamb of God, Son of the Father,
That takest away the sins of the world, have mercy upon us.
Thou that takest away the sins of the world, receive our
    prayer.
Thou that sittest at the right hand of God the Father,
Have mercy upon us. For thou only art holy;
Thou only art the Lord; thou only, O Christ, with the Holy
    Ghost,
Art most high in the glory of God the Father. Amen.

CREDO

I believe in one God the Father Almighty, Maker of heaven
    and earth,
And of all things visible and invisible;
And in one Lord Jesus Christ, the only begotten Son of God;
Begotten of his Father before all worlds,
God of God, Light of Light, Very God of Very God;
Begotten, not made; Being of one substance with the Father;
By whom all things were made:
Who for us men and for our salvation came down from heaven,
And was incarnate by the Holy Ghost of the Virgin Mary,
And was made man: And was crucified also for us under
    Pontius Pilate;
He suffered and was buried:

And the third day he rose again according to the Scriptures:
And ascended into heaven, And sitteth on the right hand of the
Father:
And he shall come again, with glory, to judge both the quick
and the dead;
Whose kingdom shall have no end. And I believe in the Holy
Ghost,
The Lord, and Giver of Life, Who proceedeth from the Father
and the Son;
Who with the Father and the Son together is worshipped and
glorified;
Who spake by the Prophets: And I believe one Catholic and
Apostolic Church:
I acknowledge one Baptism for the remission of sins:
And I look for the Resurrection of the dead:
And the Life of the world to come. Amen.

SANCTUS

Holy, Holy, Holy, Lord God of hosts,
Heaven and earth are full of thy glory:
Glory be to thee, O Lord Most High. Amen.

AGNUS DEI

O Lamb of God, that takest away the sins of the world, have
mercy upon us.
O Lamb of God, that takest away the sins of the world, have
mercy upon us.
O Lamb of God, that takest away the sins of the world, grant
us thy peace.

LISTENING TECHNIQUES

In listening to polyphonic music, keep in mind that you are
listening to melodies, not harmonies. Think of these melodies
as moving horizontally. The well-known "round" is a simple
melodic song-form that somewhat resembles polyphonic music
New or repeated tunes, entering at various intervals, usually
start with considerable emphasis or accent. If you listen for
these entrances you will find it rather easy to recognize melodic lines as they appear. Very often you will find that each

voice (soprano, alto, tenor and bass) will be singing parts that, when heard separately, are good, expressive melodies. In polyphonic music, however, you will find portions that are chordal in structure — one definite melody supported by harmony.

Suggested Renaissance Music:

Giovanni Palestrina (c. * 1524-1594)(Italian). The greatest of the old Catholic Church composers.

"Missa Papae Marcelli" (Mass for Pope Marcellus)

Other Choral works

"Masterpieces of Music before 1750" published by the Haydn Society, Inc.

Other Renaissance composers for those interested in exploring are:

Guillaume Dufay (c. 1400-1474)(Burgundian)

Heinrich Isaac (1450-1517)(German)

Josquin des Pres (c. 1450-1521)(Flemish)

Thomas Tallis (c. 1505-1585)(English)

Orlandus Lassus (c. 1525-1594)(Flemish)

Luis da Vittoria (c. 1548-1611)(Spanish)

Heinrich Schutz (1585-1672)(German) lived during the Baroque period but wrote in Renaissance style.

---

*c. — actual dates are unknown and those given are approximate.

5

Baroque

(1600-1750)

WHAT IS BAROQUE MUSIC?

The term "Baroque" (probably derived from the Portuguese word "barroco" — meaning an irregularly shaped pearl) originally implied a sort of excessively grand style in poor taste. A re-evaluation, however, is necessary because music of this period cannot be described as being in poor taste. Most of the arts have adapted the term to indicate the developments that took place during the 17th century, and the early part of the 18th century.

Practically all Baroque music is serious. It is not emotional as we think of 19th-century music, and certainly it is never sentimental. The main composers, Bach and Handel, did not invent but rather perfected forms of various kinds. Orchestral, vocal and keyboard music will be discussed.

Baroque music is often polyphonic like that of the Renaissance, but goes a step farther in some cases and becomes "contrapuntal." By "contrapuntal" (which means having counterpoint) we mean that the melodies in the polyphonic structure have distinctive significance. For example, if it were possible to play the melodies of "Star Spangled Banner" and "Marseillaise" simultaneously, and sound good, that would be "counterpoint."

Compositions by leading composers of this period have regular rhythm, ranging from delicate accents in harpsichord music to a strong driving rhythm in orchestral compositions and large vocal works such as Handel's "Messiah."

Homophonic music (music with a single melody, accompanied) became an important part of the literature of the period. These melodies generally have great strength and depth of emotional feeling. We find great joy expressed in the melody of "My Spirit Be Joyful," from Bach's "Easter Cantata," No. 146, and great sorrow expressed in the melody of "Crucifixus," from his "Mass in b minor."

A melody in Baroque instrumental music has the same strength of character that is found in vocal music. It is often "discussed" to quite some length. That is to say, the melody is not repeated over and over again identically, but changes somewhat, yet retains the same general character or spirit throughout a section of a composition or throughout the entire piece.

Baroque music is not as difficult to listen to as its reputation would have us believe. Repeated listening will give you a sense of security and a sort of "at home" feeling. Some listeners very quickly become enthusiastic about Baroque music. If you are one of these, do not hesitate to try any of the suggestions listed.

As a guide, the following may be considered an outline of the general characteristics of Baroque music:

1. Primarily serious — emotionally suppressed.
2. Polyphonic and homophonic.
3. Clear, distinct, well-defined melodies.
4. Strong to bold, driving, regular rhythm.

If you know more or less what to expect of music, you will be a little better prepared to enjoy it. The following discussions of the different kinds of Baroque music are designed to act as a guide for that purpose.

BAROQUE INSTRUMENTAL MUSIC

The Baroque Orchestra

The Baroque orchestra was made up of a mixture of ancient instruments and those that were like or similar to those used today. Some instruments used in the orchestra during this period have since been discarded. Various antiquated stringed instruments were more or less duplicates in timbre

27

or tone color. Beside the string choir there were very few other instruments. These were very different from each other in timbre — e.g., flute, oboe and trumpet.

The orchestral compositions of this period lack "color" as we think of it today. Although there is a great deal of homophonic music, the general style of writing was polyphonic. The composers took advantage of the instruments available that varied in timbre by using them to bring out the melodic lines of the polyphonic structure. In other words two melodies, one by the flute and another by an oboe, going on at the same time, are easy to follow because of the difference in the tone quality of the two instruments. (See Renaissance listening techniques.)

The typical Baroque orchestra was made up of some or all of the following instruments.

String Choir	Wood-Wind Choir	Brass Choir	Percussion
Violino Piccolo	Flute	Trumpet	Drum
Violin	Recorder	Horn	Kettle-drums
Viola	Oboe		
Violoncello	Bassoon		
Double-bass			
Harpsichord			

The violino piccolo is like a small violin but tuned higher. It has much less volume than the other stringed instruments. Its tone quality may be described as being like a slightly muted violin and a bit nasal.

Some Baroque flutes had keys, others were without them. Keys for the flute were invented in 1677.

The recorder is an end-blown instrument sounding somewhat like a flute but with a slightly reedy quality. It played an important part in the music of the Renaissance. It was used very little after 1750 and its present day revival may be termed a sort of novelty, employed by those who wish to perform Baroque music in a more authentic manner.

The kettle-drums were not used very often. They were used by Bach in his cantatas only.

Of course we have the age-old question which has no answer, "Would a Baroque composer have used other kinds of instruments if they had been available?" Many Bach numbers have been orchestrated for modern orchestra. These have great merit for the beginner and would bear investigating.

The Suite for Orchestra

The Baroque suite is made up of a group of antique dances. The interest is sustained through variety. The only unifying element is that all the dances or movements are in the same key. Sometimes, as in all the Bach suites for orchestra, the first number is an overture. Originally the overture was intended as a greeting for royal visitors, the first portion or section of the overture being rather stately, the second a little gay, and the third a return to stately character.

Bach was not an innovator, but when he set out to work in any established form, his compositions always seemed to surpass in quality those of his predecessors or contemporaries.

In his suites for orchestra, he not only amalgamated all previous styles but gave them fine melodies along with solid harmonic and polyphonic texture. These are characteristics that are quite largely responsible for their continued success. They are perennial favorites with learned and unlearned alike.

For those who want attractive Baroque orchestral numbers, the Bach suites are to be recommended. Of the four he wrote, numbers three and four are preferred because of the greater variety of instruments used. Bach's orchestra was a small one, but for those who are not sticklers for tradition, performances by the larger orchestras of today are to be recommended for the beginner.

Suggested Baroque Suites for Orchestra:

Bach: Suite No. 3 for Orchestra (see Ballet page 55)

Overture, Air, Gavotte, Bourree, Gigue.

Scored for 3 trumpets, drums, 2 oboes, violins I and II, viola, violoncello and harpsichord.

Bach: Suite No. 4 for Orchestra

Overture, Bourree, Gavotte, Menuetto, Rejouissance.

Scored for 3 trumpets, drums, 3 oboes, 2 bassoons, violins I and II, viola and violoncello.

Handel: Water Music

> The complete suite is made up of twenty-two short numbers. There is great variety in tempo and instrumentation. Handel uses many different combinations of strings, brass, and wood winds in the various movements which include some 17th-century dances.

The Baroque Solo Concerto

The Baroque solo concerto is a composition with considerable polyphonic treatment, written for solo instrument and orchestra. In its strictest sense it is not a solo with accompaniment but a piece with a unified feeling between orchestra and solo instrument — a sort of "working together." Most Baroque solo concertos are in three movements. The first and last movements are usually fast and the second, slow.

The solo concerto is one of the easiest instrumental types of the period for the listener because his attention is continually being focused on the solo instrument.

Suggested Baroque Solo Concertos:

Bach: Violin Concerto No. 2 in E Major (For the serious student only)

Corelli: Concerto for Oboe and String Orchestra (Comparatively short — delightful)

Gluck: Concerto for Flute and Chamber Orchestra in G Major (Very pleasant listening)

Handel: Twelve Organ Concertos, Op. 4 and Op. 7 for Pipe Organ and Chamber Orchestra (Lovers of early organ music should not overlook these gems.)

The Baroque Concerto Grosso

The Concerto Grosso differs from the solo concerto in that there is a group of solo instruments against the full orchestra which is made up primarily or entirely of strings.

The solo group is called "concertino" and the entire orchestra is called "tutti" or "ripieno."

Do not expect to find developments of subjects such as appear in abundance in the classic period. Instead there is considerable "conversation" between the solo group and the whole orchestra — sometimes the solo group, or one of them, will be heard alone — sometimes the main orchestral body will be heard by itself — then at times all the solo instruments and the orchestra will be playing at the same time. Many sudden changes in dynamics are typical, and many extended passages in the same volume are to be found.

Suggested Baroque Concerti Grossi:

Bach: Brandenburg Concerto No. 5

> (String orchestra with flute, violin and harpsichord as solo instruments — for Baroque enthusiasts only)

Corelli: Christmas Concerto, Op. 6, No. 8 in g minor

> (String orchestra)

Pergolesi: Concertino No. 2 in G Major

> (String orchestra)

Vivaldi: The Four Seasons (Four Concerti Grossi)
These are named "Spring," "Summer," "Autumn" and "Winter." They are outstanding examples of early orchestral program music. See page 55.

Baroque Organ Music

The Baroque organ is quite like the Baroque orchestra in that it often has timbre similar to the Baroque wood wind and brass choirs (see the outline of instruments on page 28). Consequently the organ music of this period follows very closely the tone color of baroque orchestral music. An organist chooses a registration made up of various ranks such as strings, flutes, oboes, etc., that are quite different from each other in timbre so that he may bring out melodic lines clearly and distinctly.

31

The Fugue

A fugue is a contrapuntal composition with a certain number of tunes called subjects — usually three or four. The main subject is introduced in one position (either soprano, alto, tenor or bass) and then appears in another, while a second subject is played with it. At the end of this a third subject may be added and so on, according to certain rules.

The beginning of Bach's "Fugue in g minor" from the "Fantasia and Fugue in g minor" (The Great) for organ, is outlined below. The numbers represent the subjects and show the positions where they are heard.

```
1. - - - - - -   2. * * * * * *   3. # # # # # #   4. ' ' ' ' ' '
                 1. - - - - - -   2. * * * * . * *   3. # # # # # #
                                 1. - - - - - -   2. * * * * * *
                                                 1. - - - - - -
```

In this fugue, the first tune that you hear is the main subject, or subject number one. When this is finished, a second subject starts in where the first one left off, and the first one starts again, but this time it is below the second subject as an alto part. When the third subject is added, subject number one becomes the tenor; the second subject becomes the alto and subject number three is the new soprano, etc.

The entire section outlined above is the first exposition of this fugue. Any section of a fugue, in which the main subject appears in all positions or voices, is called an exposition.

The following is an outline of the exposition of the "Little Fugue in g minor." Compare this with the exposition of "The Great Fugue in g minor" outlined above.

```
1. - - - - - -   2. * * * * * *   3. # #     4. ' '
                 1. - - - - - -   2. * * * * * *   3. # #
                                 1. - - - - - -   2. * * * * *
                                                 1. - - - - -
```

It is easy to understand the pattern of the exposition of the "Great Fugue" because it conforms to a regular plan. However, it is easier to follow the "Little Fugue in g minor" when listening to it. In the "Little Fugue" we have a feeling of the same sort of exposition that we have above, except that it has but two important tunes or subjects, a main subject and a secondary one. The places where subjects 3 and 4 appear in the "Great Fugue," are filled with less important tunes. These drop out after a short time. These tunes are polyphonic ideas, added to help make the two subjects a part of a greater drama, with more characters, than like a play with but two characters.

First expositions in fugues do not always follow this scheme. Part of the pattern may be inverted, shortened, augmented or numerous other changes made. All expositions are similar in that the main subject appears successively in all the positions or voices.

Some sections of the fugue are made up of different polyphonic melodies. These episodes, or connecting passages add variety and new interest. They also help tie the subjects together just as secondary actors in a play help tie together the main activities of the plot.

Listening to Fugues

In listening to a fugue, the most important parts to get acquainted with are the main subject and the first exposition. If a fugue is well played the main subject will be easy to recognize and follow as it appears from time to time. It is not always present any more than the main character is in a play. It may not always be played in full — only parts or fragments of it may appear here and there.

As you get a little better acquainted with the main subject of any fugue, you will be able to hear another melody that is being played while the main one is going on. Listen to two simultaneous melodies as you would look at two pictures printed from a film with a double exposure. After you are able to hear two or more melodies at once, you will find it much easier to listen to and enjoy other fugues that you do not know or know as well.

Once you get well acquainted with a fugue you will find that the "mental gymnastics" required to follow the subjects become easier and listening to them becomes fascinating.

Suggested Baroque Organ Fugues (in this order for the beginner):

Bach: Little Fugue in g minor

Bach: Toccata and Fugue in d minor

33

Bach: Fantasia and Fugue in g minor (The Great)

Bach: Prelude and Fugue in E flat Major (St. Anne)

The Baroque Chorale Prelude

The term "Chorale" is an old reformation name given to a song to be sung by the church congregation in the language of the people. A "Chorale Prelude" is an organ composition based on the tune of a "Chorale."

There are many different kinds of Chorale Preludes. Some present the melodies unaltered with interesting and varied accompaniments, others are almost like variations, and others seem to hide the melody with a great deal of polyphonic material.

Sometimes these Chorale Preludes are used at the very beginning of the church service and lead directly into the congregational singing of the same Chorale. They were originall designed for this purpose and to acquaint the congregation witl the hymn of the day. This idea of the Chorale Prelude was no new but rather a perfected form or outgrowth of the earlier organ Latin hymns, developed under the auspices of the Roma Catholic Church.

Suggested Baroque Chorale Preludes:

Bach: Jesu, Joy of Man's Desiring

Bach: Sheep May Safely Graze

Bach: Sleepers Awake

Bach: Jesus, My Joy

Bach: Christ, We Shall Praise

Bach: My Heart Is Filled With Longing

Harpsichord Music

Although the piano in its earliest stages of development w in existence during the Baroque period it is not to be conside a Baroque instrument. Most of the keyboard compositions of the period were written with the harpsichord in mind — not the piano. The suggested numbers that follow are available on records, played on either the harpsichord or the piano.

Suggested Baroque Harpsichord Music:

Bach: Partita No. 1, in B flat

> This is a delightful suite that is made up of a Prelude and antique dances: Allemande, Courante, Saraband, Two Minuets and Jig.

Bach: Well-tempered Clavichord
Handel: Harmonious Blacksmith

> This is in the form of theme and variations — a very charming harpsichord solo.

BAROQUE VOCAL MUSIC

The Church Cantatas of Bach

There is no "typical" Bach cantata. They are made up of various vocal forms — choruses, solos, duets, etc. Some may be made up entirely of choruses, others made up almost entirely of solos. Some choruses may be in four-part harmony like a hymn, others in the polyphonic style of the Renaissance. Some solo parts are easy to sing, others are very difficult and require considerable vocal training. All the Bach cantatas have orchestral accompaniments.

Bach wrote about three hundred church cantatas. The texts in most of the approximately two hundred sacred cantatas that remain in existence today are appropriate for particular Sundays of the year, such as Advent, Christmas, Epiphany, Lent, Palm Sunday, Easter, etc. The Sunday services of Bach's time were very long. They thought nothing of having a cantata every Sunday. In fact, preparing a different cantata for every Sunday of the year was required of Bach in his position in Leipzig where he was organist and director of music at Thomaskirche and Nicolaikirche. Some of these cantatas are long but most of them average about twenty-five minutes in length.

Bach's devotion to his church and his firm belief in Christianity are reflected in his church cantatas. He was a firm believer in the redemption of the world through Christ's sacrifice on the cross. In listening to Bach's cantatas the theological aspect should always be considered. Note the sincerity, enthusiasm and the depth of feeling in the music.

Suggested Church Cantatas:

Bach: Cantata No. 4, "Christ Lag in Todesbanden." (Easter Day)

Bach: Cantata No. 76, "Die Himmel Erzaehlen Die Ehrf Gottes." (For the second Sunday after Trinity)

Bach: Cantata No. 106, "Gottes Zeit" (God's Time). (Funeral Cantata)

Bach: Cantata No. 140, "Wachet Auf" (Sleepers Wake). (For 27th Sunday after Trinity)

The Oratorio

The Oratorio is a much more pretentious work than the cantata. It is very much longer, usually with a religious stor or libretto, made up of choruses, solos and duets with orches tral accompaniment. Like the cantata it is designed to be su without costumes, scenery or action, in a church (but not a p of the service) or concert hall.

Suggested Baroque Oratorios:

Carissimi: Jepthe (rather short for an oratorio — Latin text)

Handel: Messiah (very long — in English)

Baroque Operas

Suggested Baroque Operas:

Gluck*: Orfeo ed Euridice (1762) (best for the beginner

*Christoph Willibald Gluck (1714-1787) is not truly a Baroque compo but a pre-Classicist. His "Orfeo and Euridice" is the oldest opera enjoy current performances. Others of this period are seldom give only an occasional revival.

Suggested Baroque Operas: (continued)

    Handel: Julius Caesar

    Monteverdi: L'Incoronazione di Poppea

    Purcell: Dido and Aeneas

Other Outstanding Baroque Choral Works
(not for the beginner):

Bach: Mass in b minor

Bach: St. Matthew Passion

6
Rococo
(1700-1775)

During the eighteenth century, delicate ornamentation emphasizing elegance, appeared in paintings, furniture, chandeliers, etc. This movement in the arts became known as "Rococo," a term derived from the French word "Rocaille," which means shell or shellwork.

Rococo music is a sort of transition between the Baroque and the Classic art of Haydn, Mozart and the early composition of Beethoven. It is a departure from the grandeur of the Baroque emphasizing simplicity. Rococo composers wrote music that was basically graceful and charming with qualities of prettiness, pleasantness and elegance. Some of the early works of Haydn may be classified as Rococo. See list of harpsichord concertos at the top of page 50.

Although, to the average listener, music of this period is not important, the Sonatas of Dominico Scarlatti (1685-1757) should not be overlooked. They are charming little pieces written for harpsichord but often played on the piano. They vary in mood, tempo and dynamics. Each Sonata has a sense of completeness just as other short compositions for piano or harpsichord. The Sonata of this period should not be confused with the "Classic Sonata." See Glossary.

Other Rococo composers that may interest the explorer:

Bach, C.P.E. (1714-1788)

Couperin, Francois (1668-1733)

Rameau, Jean Philippe (1683-1764)

7

Classic Period
(1750-1825)

THE SYMPHONY ORCHESTRA COMES INTO BEING

The Viennese Classicists — Joseph Haydn (1732-1809), Wolfgang Amadeus Mozart (1756-1791), and Ludwig van Beethoven (1770-1827) — owe a great deal to J. W. A. Stamitz (1717-1757). It was Stamitz who standardized the symphony orchestra at the court at Mannheim, Germany, dividing it into four choirs: (1) strings, (2) wood winds, (3) brasses and (4) percussion.

The Mannheim School, under the leadership of Stamitz, was the first to explore the possibilities and use of the crecendo (gradual increase in volume), the diminuendo (gradual decrease in volume) and various shadings to make music more expressive.

We are indebted to Joseph Haydn for organizing and establishing the symphony orchestra as we think of it today. He discarded many ancient instruments and organized the orchestra in choirs after the pattern of Stamitz. None of the instruments that he discarded appeared again in the symphony orchestra.

Mozart was the first to introduce the clarinet into the orchestra. Haydn approved of the instrument and later used it in his "London" and "Clock" symphonies.

Although Mozart wrote for the harpsichord, the piano took its place in his major keyboard compositions. The Classicists used the keyboard instrument as a solo instrument and not as part of the orchestra.

The trombone was used by Gluck in his opera "Alceste,"

and by Mozart in his operas "The Magic Flute" and "Don Giovanni." Beethoven was the first to use it in a symphony.

Haydn and Mozart symphonies were written for some or all of the following instruments:

Strings	Wood Winds	Brass	Percussion
Violins	Flutes	Trumpets*	Timpani
Violas	Clarinets	Horns*	(Kettle-drum
Violoncellos	Oboes	(French Horns)	
Double-basses	Bassoons		
		*(Without valves until 1813. See page 54)	

These were the instruments that Beethoven used in his Symphonies Nos. 1, 2, 3, 4, 7 and 8. The orchestra was enlarged a little for his Fifth and Sixth Symphonies and greatly enlarged for his Symphony No. 9. Compare the above list of instruments with the list required by Beethoven for his Symphony No. 9, which is scored for chorus, solo voices and the following instruments:

Strings	Wood Winds	Brass	Percussio
1st Violins	1 Piccolo	4 Horns	2 Timpani
2nd Violins	2 Flutes	2 Trumpets	Triangle
Violas	2 Oboes	3 Trombones	Cymbals
Violoncellos	2 Clarinets		Bass Dru
Double-basses	2 Bassoons		
	1 Contrabassoon		

CHARACTERISTICS OF MUSIC OF
HAYDN, MOZART AND BEETHOVEN

Haydn and Mozart presented the emotional in music with dignified reserve and charm, approaching climaxes with considerable restraint, and wrote melodies that are quite songli and easy to listen to. Their orchestral compositions were written in clear, transparent style and in traditional forms t are easily comprehended. They wrote for sophisticated audi ences, mostly for courts, and with a few exceptions, their

40

instrumental music was absolute. Absolute music is music in which the composer presents various more or less indescribable moods that have no literary or pictorial association.

The characteristics of instrumental music of Haydn and Mozart in outline form may be more easily comprehended as follows:

1. Emotion — reserved, in moderation
2. Melodies — songlike
3. Climaxes — restrained
4. Orchestration — transparent
5. Forms — clear, well-defined
6. Primarily absolute

The characteristics of the music of Haydn and Mozart may well apply to the music of Beethoven except that in Beethoven's later compositions (those written after 1800), which include all of his symphonies, there is much less restraint in emotion and climaxes. This later period of Beethoven marks a sort of transition from pure Classicism to Romanticism.

THE SYMPHONY — A SONATA

J. W. A. Stamitz, along with C. P. E. Bach and J. C. Bach (two sons of Johann Sebastian Bach), pioneered the classic sonata. The classic sonata was brought to a high level of development by Haydn, Mozart and more especially Beethoven.

The sonata is a structural form for solo instruments such as the piano or violin, two instruments such as a sonata for violin and piano, also for groups of instruments such as a trio, quartet, quintet, etc., up to and including the symphony. The symphony is a sonata for symphony orchestra. A sonata for a trio, quartet, etc., is called "Trio," "Quartet," etc.

The typical sonata is composed of four movements or independent sections, named by tempo terms such as are listed in Italian Terms for Speeds. Choices of terms vary but the general scheme of the four movements is as follows:

First movement (fast) — Contrasting themes but in general quite cheerful and spirited.

Second movement (slow) — Songlike, lyrical, melodic.

Third movement (medium fast) — Dancelike.

41

Fourth movement (fast) — Usually full of vitality, ending with a "lift."

ANALYSIS OF BEETHOVEN'S
FIFTH SYMPHONY

This symphony has been chosen for analysis because it is generally accepted as a standard of form.

Beethoven's Fifth Symphony would be programmed as follows:

Symphony No. 5 in C Minor, Op. 67 . . . Beethoven

Allegro con brio

Andante con moto

Allegro

Allegro maestoso

The four movements are in the following forms:

Allegro con brio (1st movement) — Sonata-Allegro form

Andante con moto (2nd movement) — Two themes and variations

Allegro (3rd movement) — in Ternary form

Allegro maestoso (4th movement) — Sonata-Allegro form

Allegro Con Brio

The Sonata-Allegro form may have as many as five subdivisions. They are as follows:

(1) Introduction
(2) Exposition — main themes are introduced
(3) Development — a sort of unfolding of thematic materi
(4) Recapitulation — restatement of themes
(5) Coda — a sort of conclusion or "epilogue"

The introduction or the coda, or both, may be omitted. In this particular movement, the introduction is omitted. In the Sonata-Allegro form, as in all other forms, we find little

42

changes here and there as in houses that fulfill the same general requirements.

There is a perfect union between form and content in the Sonata-Allegro form. Melodies appear and reappear in orderly fashion as logically and appropriately as the characters appear and reappear in a drama. As an aid to listening it is well to acquaint yourself with the first melodies or tunes that you hear. These melodies or tunes are going to reappear from time to time. They may reappear slightly altered, just as characters reappear in a play wearing different costumes.

The first movement is made up primarily of two themes called First Theme and Second Theme, or Principal Theme and Subordinate Theme. The very first four notes that you hear in Beethoven's Fifth Symphony make up the first theme. This theme is repeated immediately in a slightly lower position. Then in rapid succession you will hear it repeated over and over in still different pitches, seeming to tumble over itself. This sort of "play of the theme" goes on for a while till we come to the transition which is a sort of "episode" leading us into the second theme. The second theme appears to be slower and is quite different in character.

The following is an outline of the Sonata-Allegro form with discussions of the various parts of the first movement of Beethoven's Fifth. Notice how the composer develops a musical drama with symmetry and balance.

Sonata-Allegro form —

I. Exposition (the main subjects are introduced)

    1. First Theme

    2. A Transition

    3. Second Theme

    4. Codetta (a semiending) — In this case it terminates with repetition marks which indicate that the entire exposition is to be repeated. This repetition, often called "recapitulation," is sometimes omitted, especially in records where time is to be considered.

II. Development (a sort of unfolding of the thematic material)

1. Here the composer has a chance to exercise originality and artistry in the treatment of themes by modification, inversion, counterpoint, new combinations, changes in orchestration, etc. In this symphony we hear considerable manipulating of the first theme.

2. New and contrasting material is made up of a fragment of the introductory phrase that precedes the second theme in the Exposition. This is presented in a series of sequences and adds variety. Beethoven not only creates new interest in this way but also devises ways of returning to the first theme which appears at the very beginning of the Recapitulation which follows.

III. Recapitulation or Reprise (restatement of themes)

1. Restatement of the First Theme. Here Beethoven places the theme in the bass against the full orchestra.

2. Note the very short unrelated oboe solo after the restatement of the first theme and brief reiterations of it. This not only adds variety but new interest. If we were to have exact repetitions of themes in this section it would become very dull listening. As it is there is always something that brings freshness.

3. The Second Theme transposed. Placing the second theme in a new key helps give it a feeling of "newness" since every key has a different tonal color or characteristic.

IV. Coda (conclusion)

1. With the use of old or new material any composition may be brought to a conclusion with a coda which creates a final ending. In some cases it is a sort of "epilogue" such as a concluding speech by an actor at the end of a play.

2. Codas vary in length from very short to very long. It depends on whether or not the composer wants to drive home a point, have time to build up to a climax or other dramatic effects.

Andante Con Moto

The second movement is in the form of theme and variations. A "Theme and Variations" is just about what the title would indicate — a theme or tune first presented rather simply and then changed in various ways as it appears from time to time. It is not necessary to go into detail about the endless ways that a theme may be varied. Think of variations as you would a character in a play who, every time he appears, is in a different frame of mind.

First let us dispose of the "Subordinate Theme" in the "Andante con moto." It is mentioned here because analysts have seen fit to call it a "Subordinate Theme." It appears a little over half way through the movement and is about forty-five seconds long. It can be very easily mistaken for fragments of the "Principal Theme." It is quite possible that Beethoven never intended it to be a Subordinate Theme — perhaps an episode, like a minor character appearing very briefly in a scene of a drama. For the purpose of listening casually to this movement, ignore the second theme completely.

To follow the entire construction, refer to Work Sheet No. 2. The Principal Theme is in two parts. The very first tune that you hear is Part I. It is slow, short and songlike. The little phrases, or the short "echo" passage that follows, appear first in the string choir, then the wood-wind choir. Part II of the Principal Theme then appears in the clarinets. In the Work Sheet II — 1st period and II — 2nd period the tune is approximately the same. Note that sometimes the tune is very evident — sometimes it is a little obscure.

Allegro

The third movement is in ternary form. It is made up of two sections — "A" and "B." The pattern is A-B-A. This establishes a certain sense of balance. The first "A" — Principal Section (outline page 46) is a Rondo, a-b-a-b-a.

The three terms Rondo, Rondo Form and Rondo-Sonata Form mean the same thing. For the sake of convenience we shall refer to this form as the Rondo. With letters used to name the sections, as in the ternary form above, in the rondo we may have a construction such as A-B-A-B-A, A-B-A-C-A or R-A-R-B-R-A-R. In the last, the "R" represents the

"Rondo theme." There are many more possible patterns. The general idea is to give the composition balance and symmetry. These forms are frequently used in one or more movements of the classical sonatas, symphonies and concertos.

In the following outline of the third movement of the Fifth Symphony, note the construction of the "A" or Principal Section When broken down, we have a rondo with the pattern A-B-A-B-A.

Listen to the melodies as you follow the outline. The "A" theme is at the very beginning — played by the cellos and double basses — and is very short. The "B" section is called "Trio" — or middle section (not a composition for three instruments or voices). The construction here is A-A-B-A-B.

The "A" or Principal Section follows in Ternary Form with a Codetta leading into the Fourth Movement without pause Note the lighter character of the themes played by the wood winds, etc.

Outline of the third movement of Beethoven's 5th Symphony

A- - -Principal Section

        a - Part I - Principal Theme - 1st period

        b - Part I - Principal Theme - 2nd period

        a - Part II - Principal Theme - 1st period

        b - Part II - Principal Theme - 2nd period

        a - Part III - Principal Theme - 1st period

        Codetta - (a sort of semiending)

B- - -Trio

        a - Part I - 1st Theme

        a - Part I - 1st Theme

        b - Part II - 2nd Theme

        a - Part III - 1st Theme

        b - Part IV - 2nd Theme

        a - Part V - 1st Theme

        Transition

A- - - -Principal Section

    a - Part I - Principal Theme - 1st period

    b - Part I - Principal Theme - 2nd period

    a - Part II - Principal Theme - 1st period

    Codetta (a semiclose leading directly into the fourth movement)

Allegro Maestoso

The fourth movement is in Sonata-Allegro Form — same as the first movement.

SYMPHONIES OF HAYDN, MOZART AND BEETHOVEN

Suggested Mozart Symphonies:

Symphony No. 32 in G Major, K. 318 (1779)

Symphony No. 36 in C, K. 425 "Linz" (1783)

Symphony No. 39 in E flat Major, K. 543 (1788)

Symphony No. 40 in g minor, K. 550 (1788)

Symphony No. 41 in C Major, K. 551 "Jupiter" (1788)

Suggested Haydn Symphonies:

Symphony No. 88 "Paris" (c. 1786)

Symphony No. 92 "Oxford" (1788)

Symphony No. 94 "Surprise" (1791)

Symphony No. 96 "The Miracle" (1791)

Symphony No. 100 "Military" (1794)

Symphony No. 101 "Clock" (1794)

Symphony No. 104 "London" (1795)

<u>Suggested Beethoven Symphonies:</u>

Symphony No. 3 in E flat, Op. 55, "Eroica"
(published in 1806)

Symphony No. 5 in c minor, Op. 67 (published in 1807)

Symphony No. 6 in F, Op. 68 "Pastorale" (published
soon after No. 5)

The "Pastorale" has programmatic content indicated by
the composer in the subtitles: "Cheerful impressions on arriv-
ing in the country," "By the brook," "Peasants merrymaking,"
"The Storm," and "The Shepherd's Hymn."

It is interesting to note that the Beethoven symphonic litera
ture is more popular in America than that of any other composer. If you are a Beethoven fan do not hesitate to try any of
his nine symphonies.

THE CLASSIC SOLO CONCERTO

The Classic Solo Concerto in its typical form has three
movements. The first movement is fast; the second, slow; the
third, very fast. Near the end, or at the end of the first movement we can expect a cadenza.

A cadenza is a section played by the solo instrument. It
varies in length. In the classic concertos it is usually quite
long, especially in the Beethoven concertos. It is in free
style and is virtuoso in character. Here the solo artist has a
chance to display his technical skill. The subject material is
usually from themes of the movement, interspersed with new
ideas. Many times it serves as a coda with a lot of "fireworks

The Classic Piano Concerto

The piano is an excellent solo instrument with orchestra.
Its timbre or tone color is so different from the orchestra; its
power of dynamics so variable from very soft to very loud; it
can give meaning to the daintiest passages of Mozart and the
most thunderous and dramatic episodes of Beethoven. The
piano concerto has always been popular ever since it was first
introduced during the classic period.

Mozart's piano concertos and Beethoven's piano Concerto No. 1 are to be recommended for those who are looking for refinement, grace and classic charm. Beethoven's Piano Concertos Nos. 3, 4 and 5 are quite Romantic in character and are also more dramatic.

Suggested Classic Piano Concertos:

Mozart: Concerto No. 20, K. 466

Mozart: Concerto No. 23, K. 488

Mozart: Concerto No. 27, K. 595

Beethoven: Concerto No. 1, Op. 15

Beethoven: Concerto No. 3, Op. 37

Beethoven: Concerto No. 4, Op. 58

Beethoven: Concerto No. 5, Op. 73, "Emperor"

The Classic Violin Concerto

The violin concertos of the Classic period are perhaps a little more restrained than the piano concertos. They lend themselves a little more to the intimacy that one expects of a string orchestra or a string quartet. Acquaint yourself with a Mozart violin concerto and enjoy the charm of this form of musical expression.

Suggested Violin Concertos:

Mozart: Concerto No. 4, in D, K. 218

Mozart: Concerto No. 5, in A, K. 219

Beethoven: Concerto for Violin and Orchestra, Op. 61

Suggested Miscellaneous Concertos:

These concertos are delightful and refreshing. They are not profound. For sheer pleasure, the following are recommended.

Beethoven: Concerto for Violin, Cello, Piano and Orchestra, Op. 56

Haydn: Concertos for Harpsichord in D Major,
G Major and F Major. (These harpsichord
concertos are Rococo art at its best.)

CLASSIC CHAMBER MUSIC

Chamber music is just about what the name implies —
music for a small group of instrumentalists, intended to be
performed for small audiences, in rather intimate surroundings — not in a large concert hall.

Chamber music is dignified — never boisterous. It does
not have the great masses of tone color that we expect of an
orchestra but is about the most intimate and charming form
of expression in all music literature.

The melodic lines are easy to follow and, for the most
part, the forms are easily comprehended. The movements
vary in tempo and character, giving the whole composition a
sense of completeness — a little concert in itself. There is
nothing more relaxing for the music lover than a bit of chamber music that he has become well acquainted with. Listening
to records of chamber music in your own home is a very
pleasant addition to gracious living.

The compositions suggested below are for three, four or
five instruments. If you are not acquainted with chamber
music or feel a little strange in this field of listening, we suggest trying Mozart's K. 478 listed below or Beethoven's
"Archduke" Trio. The piano adds a little variety for the beginner. Mozart's "Eine Kleine Nachtmusik" must not be overlooked. It is played by either string quartet or string orchestra. It is a very delightful Serenade (K. 525), in the form of a
classic sonata. This number has always been well liked by
both performers and listeners.

Suggested Chamber Music of the Period:

Haydn: String Quartet in d minor, Op. 76, No. 2
"Quinten"

Haydn: String Quartet in C Major, Op. 76, No. 3
"Emperor"

Suggested Chamber Music of the Period: (continued)

Haydn: String Quartet in G Major, Op. 77, No. 1

Mozart: String Quartet No. 14 in G Major, K. 387

Mozart: String Quartet No. 15 in d minor, K. 421

Mozart: Quartet in g minor for Piano, Violin, Viola and Cello, K. 478

Mozart: Quintet in A Major for Clarinet, two Violins, Viola and Cello, K. 581

Beethoven: Piano Quartets (Piano and Strings)

Beethoven: String Quartets, Op. 18, Nos. 1 to 6

Beethoven: String Quartets, Op. 59, Nos. 1 to 3 "Rosoumovsky"

(The Op. 59 is more Romantic than Op. 18)

Beethoven: Trio for Violin, Cello and Piano, No. 7, Op. 97, "Archduke"

OVERTURES

For a discussion of the Overture see page 60.

Suggested Classic Overtures:

Beethoven: Coriolan, Egmont and Leonore No. 3.

Mozart: Magic Flute, Cosi Fan Tutte, Marriage of Figaro, Don Giovanni and The Abduction from the Seraglio

PIANO SOLOS

Suggested Piano Solos:

Beethoven: Sonata Op. 13, "Pathetique"

Beethoven: Sonata Op. 27, No. 2, "Moonlight"

Beethoven: Sonata Op. 57, "Appassionata"

VOCAL MUSIC

<u>Suggested Major Vocal Works of the Period:</u>

Mozart: Magic Flute, K. 620 (Opera — see page 77)

Mozart: Don Giovanni, K. 527 (Opera — see page 77)

Haydn: The Creation (Oratorio — see page 36)

Beethoven: Missa Solemnis, Op. 123

Beethoven: Mass in C Major, Op. 86

Beethoven's "Mass in C Major" is much shorter than his more mature "Missa Solemnis." They are both more Romantic than Classic in character. The "Kyrie" of the "Mass in C Major," is a high spot. The "C Major" is not as profound a work as the "Solemnis" but is very enjoyable listening for the average person who is interested in a shorter Mass.

8

Romantic Period
(1800-1900)

CHARACTERISTICS OF ROMANTIC MUSIC

The Viennese Classicists were restrained and conventional, emphasizing formal clarity in style and exercising moderation in emotion. The Romanticists of the 19th century were quite different. They emphasized the emotional and subjective possibilities of music and presented these qualities in a very accessible manner, appealing to the public concert audiences. It may be noted here that the first public concerts were held in London in 1672 and were well established in the larger cities in most of Europe at the beginning of the 19th century.

The general social revolution of the 19th century affected music as well as all of the other arts. Music became a part of the general cultural life of the people and the serious composers were thinking in terms of music for the general public. The revolt against tradition and classicism resulted in more freedom of expression.

Composers leaned toward program music, music in which they wished to portray or present some literary or pictorial idea through their music. Realism, effects that sound like something real such as wind, storm, waterfall, etc., became a type of expression in program music. Melodies became more emotionally expressive, climaxes were unrestrained and many composers paid less attention to traditional form.

Added to all of this "about face," we find a development of nationalistic tendencies throughout Europe — a revolt against following the style of the Viennese Classicists. Music truly became an expression of certain social and national groups, and attracted the attention of people in all walks of life. Some very fine music was inspired by folk songs and folk dances.

With many improvements and additions to the symphony orchestra, and innovations in general harmonic treatment, composers created much greater tone color in orchestration than the Classicists who retained clarity and transparency in all of their compositions.

The characteristics of Romantic music may be summed up as follows:

1. Emotional qualities — unrestrained
2. Melodies — more emotionally expressive than previousl
3. Climaxes — unrestrained
4. Orchestration — greater tone color than previously
5. Form — less attention to tradition
6. An abundance of program music

NINETEENTH-CENTURY ORCHESTRAL DEVELOPMENTS

During the 19th century practically all of the instruments, except the violin family, were improved and new ones were added to the orchestra. Valves for brass instruments were invented in 1813 but composers did not write for the valve horn until 1835.

The harp is an ancient instrument, dating from about 3,00 B.C. in Mesopotamia. It was used a little by Handel, Gluck, Mozart and Beethoven, but was not included very often in the symphony orchestra until it was used by Berlioz, Liszt and Wagner. The present day double action harp was first introduced in 1810. It is called double action because each pedal may be depressed to two notches, raising or lowering the pitches of different strings.

Although the English horn was invented in 1760, it was no used until in 1767 when Gluck used it in his "Alceste." However Gluck discarded it from the score later on. It appears in Rossini's "William Tell" dated 1829, and was first used in a symphony by Berlioz in his "Symphonie Fantastique" which is dated 1830.

"Tuba" is a name generally attached to the bass horn family. There are various shaped tubas for various purposes, but the tone quality of all are quite similar. There are various ranges so that some are called euphonium or tenor tuba, bombardon or bass tuba and the lower pitched bombardon or contrabass tuba. The Wagner tuba is another. It has the reputation of being the most flexible and easiest to play of all bass horns. The bass horn as such has been used ever since it was introduced in ancient Rome. Early types of bass horns were used in orchestras just before the middle of the 19th century. Shortly after the middle of the century the tuba was introduced into the orchestra.

The celesta is a four octave percussion instrument played from a keyboard like a piano. It was first introduced by Tchaikovsky in the "Dance of the Sugar Plum Fairy," in the "Nutcracker Suite," dated 1891.

The saxophone was invented in 1840. There are six members of the saxophone family ranging from a high soprano to the bass saxophone. Although not commonly found in the symphony orchestra it was employed by composers of orchestral music as early as 1844, later to be used by composers such as Saint-Saens and Bizet and more recently by Richard Strauss, Hindemith, Milhaud and Ravel.

THE SYMPHONIC TONE POEM

Through the years, previous to the Romantic period, there were a few orchestral compositions that were written with some definite program in mind. Vivaldi's "Seasons," a group of four Concerti Grossi, representing the four seasons of the year, is one of the earliest. Other types of program music that follow, such as Beethoven's "Pastoral Symphony" and "Coriolanus Overture," and Berlioz' "Symphonie Fantastique," tell stories or present descriptive moods through music.

Franz Liszt is generally given credit for being the first to present the symphonic tone poem. A Symphonic Tone Poem is an orchestral composition in free form, designed by the composer to present certain literary or pictorial ideas. In this new type of program music for symphony orchestra, Liszt wanted complete freedom — not only freedom of expression but absolutely no tie to any traditional form. As in all other music, there is a certain feeling of completeness in symphonic tone poems, but tone poems all vary in content and structure.

In listening to a tone poem, you have a great chance to use your own imagination. The composer's program is only a guide but the rest is up to you. It is quite possible that no two listeners will have the same reaction or "see" the same things.

There are so many books with fantastic programs about music, and unlimited "reading between the lines," that it is well in every case to refer to the original program of the composer, if he had one. Many times a composer just gives a composition a title and leaves all the rest to the listener. If the composer did not write down in words what he wished to present in music, it might be just as well to use your own imagination, instead of some other program as a crutch.

"LES PRELUDES" BY FRANZ LISZT

The following is a free translation of Liszt's preface to his score of "Les Preludes." It is a paraphrase on one of Alphonse de Lamartine's poems from "Meditations Poetiques."

"What is any life but a series of preludes to that unknown song whose first notes are sounded by Death? Love is the enchanted dawn of every life, but none go through this life without storm and strife. And who, when the storm rolls away, does not resign himself to pastoral calm and its pleasant life? Yet when the trumpet sounds the call, he hastens to the post of danger, that he may once more find in action, full possession of all his power."

The general purpose in both the poem and the symphonic tone poem is to present the idea that life is a prelude to eternity. In life, which has love as a constant source of inspiration we have four phases or periods through which we all seem to pass. In the preface to the score we note that (1) we are born of love, (2) we have periods of strife and anxiety, (3) we resign ourselves to fate and enjoy the pleasant things of life, and (4) yet, when called upon, we rise to our full stature to carry on the struggle.

Let us see how Liszt portrays these ideas through music. "Les Preludes" is one single, continuous composition, but is divided into four different moods, each representing a different phase of life. The introduction is marked "Andante" (rather slow) — the other sections are called "Andante Maestoso" (rather slow and majestic), "Allegro ma non troppo" (fast but not too fast), "Allegretto Pastorale" (not very fast — in rustic spirit), and "Allegro Marziale Animato" (fast with martial animation). The program is so very suggestive that these sections may well have programmatic subtitles, characteristic of the various reflections. Subtitles are inserted in the following discussion of the entire work.

Andante (Introduction)

First we hear a faint sound from plucked strings — silence — again this same soft sound. The first three notes that you hear after this, are the three notes that make up the "germinal motif," from which the entire work grows.

Andante Maestoso ("Love")

After the introduction the "germinal motif" in a burst of joy and enthusiasm, is played by the trombones, cellos and bassoons. Liszt adds to the motif to complete his main theme, which we may call the "love" theme. This theme is played by the strings and then by the French horn. Very soon a new version of the "love" theme is played by the French horn. For the sake of identifying it later let us call this the second "love" theme.

Allegro ma non troppo ("Human Aspiration")

This is ushered in with the theme in the bass, presented in a quiet, mysterious and rather ominous manner by the cellos. We are soon in the midst of a surging turmoil. There is much unrest, activity and agitation, which subsides in a few minutes and we hear again the "love" theme — this time played by the wood winds and strings.

Allegretto Pastorale ("Nature")

A new theme is presented here and may be called the "Pastoral Theme." It is a very jolly tune, rather rustic in character. Part of the theme is first played by the horn, immediately a part of it is played by the oboe, and then in full by the clarinet. This is indeed a very happy and restful section. The second "love" theme from the Andante Maestoso reappears and is played along with the "pastoral" theme. This is a good example of counterpoint — two themes played simultaneously, each having specific significance. Listen to these two themes or melodies as you would look at the two pictures printed from a film with a double exposure.

Soon the tempo accelerates and there is a fanfare of brass announcing that something important is about to happen. It is the approaching last section which is called "Immortality."

Allegro Marziale Animato ("Immortality")

The "love" theme is heard in a very militant spirit played by the trumpets and horns, answered by the trombones. This glorious ending is a grand climax to this tone poem — a thrilling musical portrayal of victory through immortality.

Suggested Symphonic Tone Poems by Nineteenth-Century Romanticists:

Dukas: Sorcerer's Apprentice

Mussorgsky: Night on Bald Mountain

Saint-Saens: Dance Macabre, Op. 40

Smetana: The Moldau

Suggested Descriptive (Tone Poem) Suites of the Period:

Mussorgsky: Pictures at an Exhibition (Orchestrated by Ravel).

Gnomes, The Old Castle, Tuileries, Bydlo, Ballet of the Unhatched Chicks, Samuel Goldenberg and Schmuyle, The Market Place, Catacombs, The Hut on Fowl's Legs, The Great Gate of Kiev.

Rimsky-Korsakov: Coq d'Or Suite (from the opera, "Golden Cockerel")

1. Introduction; King Dodon in his Palace,
2. King Dodon on the Battlefield, 3. King Dodon and the Queen of Shemakha, 4. Bridal Procession and Lamentable Death of King Dodon.

Saint-Saens: Carnival of the Animals

1. Introduction and Royal March of the Lion,

2. Cocks and Hens, 3. Wild Asses, 4. Tortoises, 5. Elephants, 6. Kangaroos, 7. Aquarium, 8. Persons with Long Ears, 9. Cuckoo in the Deep Woods, 10. The Aviary, 11. Pianists, 12. Fossils, 13. The Swan, 14. Finale.

SYMPHONIES

Two very attractive Romantic, descriptive symphonies are listed below. These follow very closely the idea of the symphonic tone poem, except that the story is divided into movements. Some hold that these are not symphonies but are descriptive suites. The composer in each case has given us a definite program.

Suggested Program Symphonies:

Berlioz: Symphonie Fantastique, Op. 14 —
subtitled "An Episode in the Life of an Artist."

There are five movements, each with a subtitle. The subtitles are: "Visions and Passions," "The Ball," "Scene in the Country," "March to the Gallows," and "Witches' Sabbath."

Goldmark: Rustic Wedding Symphony, Op. 26

"Wedding March," "Bridal Song," "Serenade," and "In the Garden."

Romanticists, although less concerned with form than the Classicists, wrote most of their symphonies in the traditional four movements. The general character of each movement usually conforms to the general ideas as set forth by the Classicists. That is, the first and last movements are generally fast and spirited, the second movement slow and lyrical, and the third dancelike. The Romanticists were much more emotional, generally less reserved, and wrote with much greater orchestral tone color than the Classicists.

The composers have not given us a descriptive program in connection with any of the symphonies listed on the following page. They are all classified as absolute music, music without pictorial or literary content.

Suggested Symphonies (absolute):

Bizet: Symphony No. 1 in C Major

Brahms: Symphony No. 1, Op. 68

Brahms: Symphony No. 4, Op. 98

Bruckner: Symphony No. 4, "Romantic"

Chausson: Symphony in B flat, Op. 20

Dvorak: Symphony No. 5, Op. 95, "New World"

Franck: Symphony in d minor

Mendelssohn: Symphony No. 4, Op. 90, "Italian"

Saint-Saens: Symphony No. 3, Op. 78, "Organ Symphony"

Schubert: Symphony No. 8, "Unfinished"

Tchaikovsky: Symphony No. 4, Op. 36

Tchaikovsky: Symphony No. 6, Op. 74, "Pathetique"

THE OVERTURE

The overture, as an independent piece, did not become a part of the orchestral concert repertoire until during the Romantic period. Overtures of the Classic and Romantic composers appear quite frequently on symphony programs today and are a very acceptable addition to these concerts. Little need be said about how to listen to these because they are all very enjoyable without guidance. However, some general ideas may be helpful in knowing what to expect of different kinds of overtures.

There are three different kinds of overtures. They are: 1. Operatic Overture — an orchestral introduction to an opera or similar work, 2. Incidental Overture — an orchestral preface to a play and 3. Concert Overture — an independent concert piece for orchestra.

There are, of course, the early overtures of the 17th century and the early 18th century that are unlike the three kinds mentioned above. The so-called "French" overture (unrelated to the work it introduced), of Jean Baptiste Lully

(1632-1687), was made up of a slow and stately movement — a fast movement in fugal style — and the slow part repeated. Some dance form of the day was often included. Originally this type of overture was intended as a salute or greeting to royal visitors. The so-called "Italian" overture (unrelated to the work it introduced) of Alessandro Scarlatti (1659-1725), was made up of a fast section — slow melodic section — ending with a fast section. The latter almost appears to be a predecessor of the classic symphony.

In a preface to "Alceste," Christopher Willibald Gluck (1714-1787) noted: "My idea was that the overture ought to indicate the subject and prepare the spectators for the character of the opera they are about to see."

Composers, after Gluck, followed his example and incorporated in their operatic overtures some of the thematic material of the opera. These portions are most often the best or "hit" tunes of the show. Because of these "hit" tunes, many overtures are still popular in orchestral concerts, while the operas for which they were written, are no longer performed.

As a whole, no matter what the Romantic overture, you can be pretty well assured of easy, pleasant listening. None of them are excessively long.

Suggested Romantic Operatic Overtures:

 Glinka: Russian and Ludmila

 Rossini: William Tell, Italiana in Algeria,
   Signor Bruschino, Cinderella, The Thieving Magpie.

 Wagner: Flying Dutchman, Tannhauser, Rienzi,
   Lohengrin.

 Weber: Euryanthe, Oberon, Freischutz.

Suggested Romantic Incidental Overtures:

 Mendelssohn: Ruy Blas, Midsummer Night's Dream.

Suggested Romantic Concert Overtures:

 Berlioz: Roman Carnival Overture, Op. 9.

 Brahms: Academic Festival Overture, Tragic Overture.

Elgar: In the South (Descriptive of joys upon visiting Italy).

Mendelssohn: Hebrides (also known as Fingal's Cave).

Rimsky-Korsakov: Russian Easter.

Tchaikovsky: Solonnelle "1812."

BALLET MUSIC

A ballet is an artistic theatrical dance, performed by a group of dancers in appropriate costumes, to the accompaniment of music. The production is usually done with fine staging, scenery and lighting effects.

The ballet, as a part of a theatrical production, dates back to the early Greek theatre. Very little is known about the music in connection with the early dance. One of the influential people to take an interest in the dance and the ballet was Louis XIV of France (1643-1717). He fostered the dance and the ballet, primarily because he himself was a great dancer. He was quite largely responsible for introducing into the court many new dance types such as the minuet, gavotte, bouree, passepied and rigaudon.

Many outstanding composers incorporated these dance types in their suites. Of notable importance are the suites of Bach which were written between the years 1717 and 1723 (see page 29).

There were many fine ballet dancers during the 18th century and many accounts of brilliant performances but little of the music has come down to us. The first important ballet music, as far as the listener is concerned, dates from the latter part of the 19th century. Leo Delibes' music for "Coppelia" is the earliest example. This ballet was first performed in 1870.

The ballet, as a complete story, is an artistic union of a story and the dance, with considerable pantomime. Tchaikovsky's "Sleeping Beauty" and "Swan Lake" are excellent examples of this type.

An opera may have a ballet as an interlude — not essentia

a part of the plot. It may be rather loosely connected with the story, but primarily serves as a diversion from the singing. An example of this type is "Dance of the Hours" from the opera, "La Gioconda" by Ponchielli.

Another type of ballet music is that which survives, while the opera for which it was written is neglected. Exciting music that falls in this category is "Le Cid" ballet music by Massenet written for his opera by the same name. This ballet suite is made up of celebrated dances of different provinces of Spain. If you like Spanish music don't overlook this one. The dances included are: Castillane, Andalouse, Argonaise, Aubade, Catalane, Marilene and Navarraise.

"Les Patineurs" (The Skaters), which Constant Lambert arranged from extracts from Meyerbeer's operas "The North Star" and "The Prophet," is equally exciting. This was first produced at the Sadler's Wells Theatre, London, 1937.

Suggested Romantic Ballet Music:

> Borodin: Polovetsian Dances, from "Prince Igor" (with chorus)
>
> Chopin: Les Sylphides (orchestrated piano pieces)
>
> Delibes: Coppelia (see comments on preceding page)
>
> Glazounov: The Seasons, Op. 67 (always popular)
>
> Massenet: Le Cid (see above comments)
>
> Meyerbeer-Lambert: Les Patineurs (see above comments)
>
> Offenbach-Rosenthal: Gaite Parisienne (arranged from several operas)
>
> Ponchielli: Dance of the Hours, from "La Gioconda"
>
> Tchaikovsky: The Nutcracker, Op. 71
>
> Tchaikovsky: Sleeping Beauty (see comments on preceding page)
>
> Tchaikovsky: Swan Lake (see comments on preceding page)

INCIDENTAL MUSIC

Incidental music is music written to be played before or during the action of a play and to assist in establishing, supporting or intensifying the mood of the drama. The term "incidental" applies to all such music, whether it be for stage, screen, radio or television.

This kind of music is not new with the Romantic period. The early Greek dramatists found it to be a very valuable part of their theatrical productions. An example of incidental music of the classic period is Beethoven's music for Goethe's "Egmont." The Romanticists were the first to write very much for the theatre that is worthy of a place in the concert repertoire.

There are three kinds of incidental music; that which precedes the show (incidental overture), played during the action of the play (incidental), and music between the acts or scenes (entr'acte or intermezzo).

Some hold that the overture and entr'acte or intermezzo are not incidental. They are placed in that category here because, after all, they do assist in establishing a mood before the show and between acts or scenes.

One of the best ways to enjoy incidental music is to associate it with that part of the play for which it was intended. However, there is much good music written for the theatre that is able to survive on its own. The popular conception or use of some incidental music has caused it to grow completely away from the show for which it was intended. For example, at a wedding, few people think of the original idea back of Mendelssohn's "Wedding March," written for Shakespeare's fantastic comedy, "Midsummer Night's Dream."

Suggested Incidental Music by Romantic Composers:

Bizet: L'Arlesienne Suites Nos. 1 and 2.

Suite No. 1 — Prelude, Minuet, Adagietto, Carillon.

Suite No. 2 — Pastorale, Intermezzo, Minuet and Farandole.

The numbers in this suite are taken from the twenty-seven pieces written for Alphonse Daudet's drama, "L'Arlesienne," which was first produced in 1872.

Grieg: Peer Gynt Suites Nos. 1 and 2.

> Suite No. 1 — Morning, Ase's Death, Anitra's Dance, In the Hall of the Mountain King.

> Suite No. 2 — Ingrid's Lament, Arabian Dance, Return of Peer Gynt, Solveig's Song.

> These pieces were written for Hendrick Ibsen's play "Peer Gynt," first produced in 1876.

Mendelssohn: Midsummer Night's Dream, Op. 21 and Op. 61.

> There are 12 pieces that Mendelssohn wrote for Shakespeare's "Midsummer Night's Dream," first produced in 1843. The most frequently heard in concert are: Overture, Scherzo, Nocturne, Intermezzo and Wedding March.

NATIONALISM IN MUSIC

Any sincere composer is influenced by his surroundings, his native countryside and all that has gone before him for generations — folk music, native dances and the general culture of his people. When a composer sets out, consciously or unconsciously, to emphasize these characteristics in his music, he may be described as a "nationalistic" composer.

To set out to describe in words the characteristics of music of the different countries would be impossible, or at least unsatisfactory. Some composers have written major compositions which we might term "nationalistic" or having "nationalistic" tendencies and yet the same composers may write with a more or less international aspect as well. These nationalistic tendencies prevailed throughout Europe during the Romantic period.

The following is a sampling of music of different countries chosen to illustrate nationalism. For the most part, each of these compositions is rather characteristic of the country that it represents. Most of them were written during the 19th century — a few were written a little later.

Suggested list of music from different countries showing national traits:

Austria — Strauss, Johann: Waltzes

Bohemia — Dvorak: Slovanic Dances

Bohemia — Smetana: The Moldau

Finland — Sibelius: Swan of Tuonela

Finland — Sibelius: Finlandia

Germany — Weber: Overture to "Der Freischutz"

Hungary — Kodaly: Intermezzo, from "Hary Janos" Suite

Norway — Grieg: Norwegian Dances, Op. 35

Spain — de Falla: Nights in the Gardens of Spain

Spain — Granados: Intermezzo from opera "Goyescas"

NATIONALISM IN RUSSIA

By western European standards, Russian music is astonishingly new. Her first important contact with western European music was during the reign of Catherine the Great (1762-1796), who dictated the policies of the court.

Catherine the Great was a Protestant Prussian princess. She wanted to surround herself with all the culture that she ha enjoyed in the Prussian court. She brought in many musicians from western Europe, including her kapellmeister, Dominico Cimarosa, who later succeeded Salieri as kapellmeister in Vienna. Classicism was established in the Russian court and furthermore it was accepted — because Catherine was Empres

Musical Classicism was so deeply rooted in the minds of the people of the Russian court that it was accepted as a stand ard of style for many years. Not until Michail Ivanovitch Glir (1804-1857) presented his opera, "A Life for the Tsar," in 18 did the Russians realize that there was a tremendous possibil for developing their own national music. Glinka's opera was not like the music that Catherine had brought to them but was

66

inspired by the people — their folk songs, their dances, their way of life.

A group of composers, known as the "Russian Five," worked together, held to their national heritage and formed a Russian national school. The "Five," Mily Balakirev (1837-1910), Nicholas Rimsky-Korsakov (1844-1908), Alexander Borodin (1833-1887), Modeste Mussorgsky (1839-1881) and Cesar Cui (1835-1918) took upon themselves the responsibility of writing true Russian music.

For many centuries Russia was in contact with oriental culture. Impressions of long standing left their mark, especially in southern Russia, and the result was that in much of the music of the "Five" we hear exotic influences. Exoticism in music may be described as musical culture not characteristically European.

Note the oriental "flavor" in the following compositions by Russians:

Borodin: Polovetsian Dances, from the opera "Prince Igor"

Rimsky-Korsakov: Scheherazade (Arabian Nights)

Ippolitof-Ivanov: In the Village, from "Caucasian Sketches"

Balakirev: Islamey (piano solo)

Cui: Orientale

Khachaturian: Lullaby, from "Gayne Ballet," Suite No. 1

ENCORES — ORCHESTRAL

Suggested Orchestral Works of the Encore Type:

Brahms: Hungarian Dances

Chabrier: España

Chabrier: Le Roi Malgre Lui (Dance Slave)

Tchaikovsky: Capriccio Italien, Op. 45

Tchaikovsky: Marche Slave, Op. 31

Tchaikovsky: Polonaise, from "Eugene Onegin"

Tchaikovsky: Waltz, from "Serenade in C,"
Op. 48

Tchaikovsky: Waltz, from "Eugene Onegin"

Wagner: Prelude to Act Three, from "Lohengrin"

ROMANTIC CHAMBER MUSIC

Romantic chamber music is a great deal like Classic chamber music (see page 50), except that it is more emotionally expressive. The tone color is the same, but the harmonic construction of the Romantic compositions tends to give them a little more lush character. Freedom from the traditional is evident in the general style and, even though chamber music is the most serene form of musical expression, unrestrained Romanticism shows through.

For a starter for the record collector, Schubert's "Trout Quintet is recommended.

Suggested Romantic Chamber Music:

Brahms: Sextet in B flat (strings), Op. 18

Brahms: Quartet No. 2 in A for Piano and Strings, Op. 2

Brahms: Quintet for Clarinet and Strings, Op. 115

Franck: Quintet in f minor for Piano and Strings

Schubert: Quartet No. 14 in d minor, "Death and the Maiden"

Schubert: Quintet for Piano and Strings, Op. 114, "Trout

FAVORITE WORKS FOR SOLO VIOLIN
AND ORCHESTRA

Brahms: Violin Concerto in D, Op. 77
Bruch: Concerto No. 1 in g minor, Op. 26
Chausson: Poem for Violin and Orchestra, Op. 25
Glazounov: Concerto in a minor, Op. 82
Lalo: Symphonie Espagnole for Violin and Orchestra

Mendelssohn: Violin Concerto in e minor, Op. 64
Paganini: Violin Concerto No. 1 in D, Op. 6
Saint-Saens: Introduction and Rondo Capriccioso, Op. 28
Sarasate: Zigeunerweisen, Op. 20, No. 1
Tchaikovsky: Concerto in D for Violin and Orchestra, Op. 35
Vieuxtemps: Concerto No. 5 in a minor for Violin and
    Orchestra, Op. 37
Wieniawski: Concerto No. 2 in d minor, Op. 22

FAVORITE CONCERTOS FOR
PIANO AND ORCHESTRA

Brahms: Piano Concerto No. 2 in B flat, Op. 83
Chopin: Piano Concerto in e minor, Op. 11
Chopin: Piano Concerto in f minor, Op. 21
Grieg: Concerto in a minor, Op. 16
Liszt: Piano Concerto No. 1 in E flat
Mendelssohn: Piano Concerto No. 1, Op. 25
Saint-Saens: Piano Concerto No. 2, Op. 22
Schumann: Piano Concerto in a minor, Op. 54
Tchaikovsky: Piano Concerto No. 1 in b flat minor, Op. 23

MISCELLANEOUS PIANO SOLOS

Brahms: Waltzes, Rhapsodies, Intermezzi
Chopin: Etudes, Scherzi, Preludes, Nocturnes, Waltzes,
    Ballades, Fantasy in f minor
Chopin: Sonatas — b flat minor and b minor
Liszt: Hungarian Rhapsodies
Schubert: Impromptus
Schumann: Carnaval, Op. 9 (suite)
Schumann: Symphonic Etudes, Op. 13

ROMANTIC ORGAN MUSIC

Brahms: Choral Preludes (11), Op. 122
Franck: Cantabile
Franck: Three Chorales for Organ
Franck: Piece Heroique
Widor: Symphonies for Organ

THE ART SONG

The Art Song is a song of the highest artistic quality. The text is usually a very fine lyric poem supported by, or fused with, a sympathetic melody and accompaniment. It is one of the greatest contributions to Romantic vocal literature. The German Art Song is called "Lied."

The Lied or Art Song has become one of the best loved vocal forms by both artist and audience. There is no small wonder when we consider that these songs are products of great poets like Goethe, Schiller and Heine, combined with melodies and accompaniments of composers like Schubert, Wolf, Schumann, Franz and Brahms. Composers like Schubert and Wolf wrote spontaneously. Their spontaneity and enthusiasm seems to show through and fires the imagination of performing artists and listeners alike.

To get a better understanding of the Art Song — what to expect and what to listen for — let us analyze it by way of the seven elements and see how the text, melody and accompaniment are related and interwoven. This will give you some specific information about the mechanics of the Art Song (see Glossary).

Rhythm

Recite any poem that you know. Notice that the poem falls into more or less regular rhythmic patterns with accents on important or key words or syllables. The meter or rhythm of the music must conform to the meter of the text so that important words will be emphasized when sung.

Melody

Generally the rise and fall of the melodic line conforms to the rise and fall of the emotional aspect of the text. For example a composer does not have a soprano sing high notes just to show off but perhaps to assist in bringing out or emphasizing an important syllable, word or phrase in the text. Notice the pitch of the human voice as it changes with the change of emotion.

Harmony

The harmony in the accompaniment is sympathetic with

he meaning and spirit of the text. There are chords that express various kinds of emotion such as sorrow or happiness.

Tempo

The tempo or speed of an Art Song is very important in
projecting the general feeling of the lyric. A poem with a joy-
ous, exciting text would require a faster speed than one of
prayer or meditation.

Dynamics

The volume (loud or soft) conforms to the mood and drama
of the text. A song about a football victory would certainly be
louder than one about a little girl singing a lullaby to her dolls.

Color

The color or quality of tone in the human voice changes
with different emotional experiences. You can recognize this
in the speaking voice. In order to sing Art Songs well, the
voice must be well trained so that the singer can go through
the whole range of emotional expression without faltering.
Those who sing Art Songs must be great actors through vocal
interpretation without physical acting.

Form

The Art Song may have one of three forms. (1) It may be
strophic — every verse has the same melody and accompaniment like a church hymn, (2) modified strophic — some verses
vary from the pattern of the first verse, or (3) "Through-
composed," in which every verse is different.

The Erlking — Schubert

Listen to Schubert's "Erlking," a setting of Goethe's poem
by the same name. A father is carrying his dying son on horse-
back — followed and haunted by the Erlking, the spirit of death.
The piano introduction at once gives us a feeling of uneasiness
and haste. The repeated notes represent the galloping of the
horse, while the quickened melodic figure in the bass represents the ominous cunning of the Erlking keeping apace with
the horse as it is urged onward into the night. The father is

71

trying to comfort the child as he hurries, trying to reach home before it is too late.

There are four characters in this drama — narrator, father, son and the Erlking. Notice how the quality of the voice of the singer changes from one character to another and how important the interpretation is in this short tragedy.

The following is a free translation of the entire poem.
The characters in this song are given here to assist the listener.

The Erlking

Narrator	Who rides so late through night and wind? It is the father with his child; He holds the boy in his arms, He holds him tightly, he keeps him warm.
Father	"My son, why do you hide your face in fear?"
Son	"Father, can't you see the Erlking? The Erlking with his crown and robe?"
Father	"My son, that is only a streak of mist."
Erlking	"Lovely child, come, go with me! Such merry games I'll play with you; Where many gay flowers bloom in the field, My mother has many golden robes."
Son	"My father, my father, can't you hear What the Erlking is whispering to me?"
Father	"Be calm, be calm, my child; That is the wind moaning through the leaves."
Erlking	"My fine boy, won't you go with me? My daughters will take care of you; My daughters will play in the evening And they will sing and dance."
Son	"My father, my father, can't you see The Erlking's daughters in that dark place?"
Father	"My son, my son, I see it quite clearly. It is only the gray willow tree."
Erlking	"I love you, your beauty arouses me; If you come not willingly I shall use force."

Son	"My father, my father, he is taking me! The Erlking has hurt me!"
Narrator	The father shudders, he rides faster, He holds the sobbing child to his bosom, He reaches home full of fear and dread — In his arms ... the child was dead!

Suggested Art Songs:

Schubert: The Erlking, Death and the Maiden,
Who is Sylvia? Ave Maria, The Trout,
Gretchen at the Spinning Wheel.

Schubert: Miscellaneous songs — settings of poems
by Goethe.

Schumann: The Two Grenadiers

Schumann: Song Collections

Wolf: Kennst du das land (Knowest thou the land)

Wolf: Song Collections

THE SONG CYCLE

A song cycle is a series of art songs having some psychological association with each other, the same general character or some general unifying thought that makes the entire collection an entity.

An understanding of and sympathetic feeling toward the text of a song cycle makes it become a living, stirring work of art. When listening to an art song or song cycle, let your imagination take over to the extent that you become a part of the experience being related or portrayed by the singer. Listen as if it were of direct concern to you.

To acquaint the reader with the possible contents of the song cycle, the titles of the individual songs of Brahms' "Vier Ernste Gesange" (Four Serious Songs), Op. 121, are listed here. They are: 1. "It befalleth both men and beasts," 2. "I journeyed on my way," 3. "Death, how bitter thou art," and 4. "Though with tongues of men and holy angels."

Suggested Song Cycles by Romantic Composers:

Berlioz: Les Nuits d'Ete, Op. 7 (Summer Nights)

Brahms: Vier Ernste Gesange, Op. 121 (Four Serious Songs)

Elgar: Sea Pictures, Op. 37 (in English)

Sea Slumber-Song

In Haven (Capri)

Sabbath Morning at Sea

Where Corals Lie

The Swimmer

Schubert: Die Schone Muellerin, Op. 25 (The Miller's Beautiful Daughter)

Schubert: Die Winterreise (Winter Journey)

Schumann: Dichterliebe, Op. 48 (Poet's Love)

Schumann: Liederkreis, Op. 39 (Song Cycle)

MISCELLANEOUS ROMANTIC CHORAL MUSIC

We cannot overemphasize the importance of familiarity and its relation to the enjoyment of music. This is especially true of some of the longer vocal works listed here. Short sketches of these, or a listing of contents are given as a guide. All of the following compositions have characteristic Romantic emotional appeal, befitting the text.

Brahms: Alto Rhapsody, Op. 53 — Contralto Solo, Male Chorus and Orchestra

The "Alto Rhapsody" is a deeply moving work. The text is taken from a portion of Goethe's somber and exciting poem "Harzreise im Winter," a story of Goethe's journey through the Hartz Mountains to visit a hermit who had sought refuge from his self-imposed withdrawal in correspondence with Goethe.

The text of the "Alto Rhapsody" is that portion of the poem which deals with loneliness and renunciation. Brahms

wrote this magnificent work with emotional understanding —
he too had a lonely existence.

Brahms: German Requiem, Op. 45

This Requiem does not conform to the accepted pattern of
the mass for the dead, as the one by Faure outlined below. In
the first place it is in German — not Latin. Brahms, it seems,
wrote this either for Robert Schumann or for his own mother.
He chose his own text from the Bible, making it a more or less
personal farewell. Like the Beethoven "Missa Solemnis," it is
suitable for concerts only — not a religious service. The work
is for Soprano Solo, Baritone Solo and Chorus. The parts of
this Requiem are as follows:

1. Blessed are they that mourn.
2. Behold, all flesh is as the grass.
3. Lord, Make me to know the measure of my days
   on earth.
4. How lovely is Thy dwelling place.
5. Ye now are sorrowful.
6. Here on earth have we no continuing place.
7. Blessed are the dead which die in the Lord.

Bruckner: Mass in e minor

This mass conforms to the traditional pattern of the choral
mass established in the early Roman Catholic Church. The
text is identical with the Renaissance Mass (see page 23), but
it is written in the style of the Romanticists. The choral parts
of this mass are as follows:

Kyrie — Lord have mercy.
Gloria — Glory be to God on high.
Credo — I believe in God.
Sanctus — Holy, Holy, Holy.
Benedictus — Blessed is he that cometh in the name of
    the Lord.
Agnus Dei — Lamb of God.

Faure: Requiem, Op. 48

The text of the Requiem is from the "Missa pro defunctis,"
the Mass for the Dead. This Requiem is a choral mass written
for the Roman Catholic Church, and can be used as such

because it is short and has the traditional text in Latin. It has the following sections:

1. Introit (Give them eternal rest) and Kyrie
2. Offertorium (accompanying the placing of the Bread and Wine on the Altar)
3. Sanctus (Holy, Holy, Holy)
4. Pie Jesu (Merciful Jesus)
5. Agnus Dei (O Lamb of God)
6. Libera Me (Deliver Me)
7. In Paradisum (In Paradise)

Mendelssohn: Elijah, Op. 70 (Oratorio)

This oratorio contains some of Mendelssohn's finest vocal writing. It has always been popular and continues to hold the attention of audiences. The text is concerned with the important episodes in the life of the prophet, Elijah. The score contains the following arias:

"If with all your hearts"
"Lord God of Abraham"
"Hear Ye, Israel!"
"O rest in the Lord"
"Then shall the righteous shine"

Verdi: Requiem Mass, "Manzoni"

This Requiem was composed in 1874 in memory of Alessandro Manzoni. It is one of the most thrilling and deeply moving religious offerings of the whole Romantic period, scored for soprano, alto, tenor and bass soloists, chorus and orchestra and written in typical Verdi operatic style. It has the following sections:

Requiem (Grant them eternal rest)

Kyrie (Lord have mercy)

Dies Irae (Day of Anger)

Tuba Mirum (Wondrous sound the trumpet flingeth)

Libera Scriptus (Now the record shall be cited)

Quid Sum Miser (What affliction mine exceeding?)

Rex Tremendae (King of Might and awe, defend me!)

Ricordare (Think, kind Jesus, my salvation)

Ingemisco (Hear my weeping and my wailing)

Confutatis (While the wicked are confounded)

Lacrymosa (What weeping on the morrow)

Offertorium: Domine Jesus (Lord, Jesus Christ!)

Sanctus (Holy, Holy, Holy)

Agnus Dei (Lamb of God)

Lux Aeterna (Light eternal shine upon them, Lord)

Liber Me (Deliver me, Lord, from eternal death)

OPERA AND OPERETTA

It is well to acquaint yourself with the different kinds of musical shows and some of the terms used in connection with them. The following are defined in the Glossary and are listed here for your convenience: Opera, Opera Buffa, Opera Bouffe, Singspiel, Opéra-comique, Comic Opera, Operetta, Musical Review, Ensemble, Aria, Recitative, Libretto and Leit-motif.

Preparing To Hear an Opera

A thorough study of the opera takes more space than is practical here. However, a few hints to the listener might be appropriate. There is much to be said in favor of good preparation on the part of the audience.

First of all it is well to have a libretto or at least to know the story ahead of time. Sometimes cuts are made, especially in long operas. If you plan to follow the libretto during the performance, you should have one of the performance that you are going to hear.

Be well-rested and well-fed before attending an opera. This is very important. A sense of well-being means a great deal to you in adding to your pleasure and enjoyment of any musical production or concert of any kind. You are more liable to be "in the mood" for good music.

If you have never seen an opera, choose one that may be easy listening. Put off the Wagner operas for some time —

they are the most difficult of all. The list of suggested operas
is intended to help those who have heard very few operas or
none at all. If you are interested in records, we suggest that
you start with albums of excerpts or concert versions. These
will give you the musical high lights and all the "favorites" of
the show. They are very pleasant, not too long and less ex-
pensive.

Opera and Operetta Compared

Opera	Operetta
1. Tragedy or comedy	1. Comedy
2. Recitatives — some spoken dialogue	2. Much more dialogue
3. Extravagant production — finest soloists, choruses, scenery, ballet, orchestra, costumes, conductors	3. Less lavish
4. Plots — fine literary, mythical, biblical or historical	4. Plots — more related to the personal experiences of the general audience

In both cases the instrumental and vocal music, the drama
acting, staging, design, costumes, etc., are in good theatrical
style.

The following 19th-century operettas or light operas are
popular perennial favorites:

Offenbach: Orpheus in Hades (1858)

Offenbach: Tales of Hoffman (1881)

Strauss, Johann: Die Fledermaus (1874)

Strauss, Johann: The Gypsy Baron (1885)

Suggested operas and the years in which they were first
produced:

Bizet: Carmen (1875)

Gounod: Faust (1859)

Suggested operas and the years in which they were first produced: (continued)

Leoncavallo: Pagliacci (1892)

Mussorgsky: Boris Godunov (1874)

Puccini: Madame Butterfly (1904)

Puccini: La Boheme (1896)

Rossini: Barber of Seville (1816)

Verdi: Aida (1871)

Verdi: La Traviata (1875)

Wagner: Die Meistersinger (1868)

9
Impressionism
(1890-1925)

INFLUENCE OF PAINTERS AND POETS

Impressionistic composers were influenced and inspired by the Impressionistic painters. These painters, such as Claud Monet, Camile Pissaro, Edgar Degas, Auguste Renoir and Edouard Manet, preferred to express their reactions or capture a fleeting glance, rather than paint with photographic precision. To do this they painted with shimmering outlines, with very little detail and often painted one color over another instead of mixing their colors. When you look at a picture painted in this manner, you get a feeling of a fleeting impression and your eyes "mix" the colors. In other words the Impressionists suggested rather than emphasized reality.

Impressionistic composers were also influenced and inspired by a literary movement called "symbolism." Symbolism deals with indefinite generalities, indirect references, subtleties and illusions. Among the symbolists were Stephane Mallarme and Paul Verlaine. The symbolists showed their aversion to Romanticism by avoiding the emotional, pathetic, tragic and great problems of life. They were concerned with lesser subjects, directed attention toward refinement and emphasized the esthetic.

CHARACTERISTICS OF IMPRESSIONISM IN MUSIC

Impressionism in music is a reactionary movement against Romanticism, especially in regard to emotional content. Like the poets, Impressionistic composers avoided excessive emotion. Like the painters, they preferred vagueness and suggestion to realism. Like both the poets and painters, they wanted to leave much to the imagination.

The two French composers, Claude Debussy (1862-1918) and Maurice Ravel (1875-1937), are generally recognized as the main representatives of Impressionism in music. From an esthetic point of view their works are quite similar but upon close examination we find that all who may be classified as Impressionists, or were influenced by the movement, wrote in quite different styles.

As a young man, Debussy was fascinated with oriental music and continued to show interest in it for some time. This may account for his many zig-zag melodies that show exotic influence. He favored the whole-tone scale (see technical characteristics on next page, while Ravel avoided it. Ravel's melodies are more definite while Debussy's are sometimes a little obscure with fragments of melody here and there. Debussy was antagonistic toward form, while Ravel was not. Ravel's orchestration is superior. He is recognized as being one of the best orchestrators of the twentieth century.

The American composer, Charles Tomlinson Griffes (1884-1920) was an Impressionist who, like Debussy, was attracted to the exotic, yet his style was a little modified with some Romanticism "showing through." Another who did not ape any of his fellow composers was the Englishman, Frederick Delius (1862-1934). He was an Impressionist who also had Romantic tendencies. His pieces are very sensitive, show considerable emotional restraint but stir the imagination.

Ottorino Respighi (1870-1936), an Italian, shows Impressionistic tendencies, but goes a step farther, writing in a more advanced 20th-century harmonic idiom in his development of orchestral tone color, which ranges from quiet, sensitive moods to the most vigorous dissonances.

Debussy, Ravel, Griffes, Delius and Respighi had a few things in common. They all avoided academic developments in music. Not one of them wrote a symphony! They avoided pathos, tragedy and emotional emphasis. Note the titles in the suggested list of music. The compositions listed are of a poetic and imaginative character, dealing with fleeting impressions, tone colors and moods ranging from the most calm to the most turbulent — from the most refined to the most boisterous.

Impressionism became an influence rather than a crusade
There are composers who, from time to time, have written
some things in an Impressionistic vein. This would not identif
them as whole-hearted or full-fledged Impressionists but woul
rather testify to the universality of the influence of the movement.

Impressionistic music may be characterized by some or
all of the following:

1. Vagueness
2. Atmosphere
3. Elusiveness
4. Successions of tone colors
5. Avoids excessive emotion

SOME TECHNICAL PHASES OF IMPRESSIONISM

The scale — Active and inactive tones — Whole-tone scales

A scale is a family of tones bearing a definite relation to
each other. Let us take the scale of C major for example. O
the piano this includes just the white keys starting with the
first white key to the left of any of the two black keys. Count-
ing this, which is named "C," as number one, play eight white
keys to the right. This is the major scale of C. Within this
family of tones we have active and inactive tones. Play the
scale once more, but stop next to the top C. This tone is
called the "leading" tone, because it is so active that it practically compels us to play C, which is called the "key note"
(home base). The leading tone is the most active of all the
tones in a major scale.

When a composer wants to come to a positive ending,
chords with active tones are chosen to precede a definite
close. When a state of suspense or atmosphere is desired,
active tones are avoided. The whole-tone scale accomplishes
this perfectly because in it there are no active tones. Start
with any key on the piano and play a scale up or down the key
board skipping every other key whether it be black or white —
this is a whole-tone scale. The octave is then divided into si
equal intervals. Listen to this scale and compare it with the
major scale. Note how inactive it is. The whole-tone scale
was a favorite with Debussy.

Color

Choose any white key on the piano — skip a white key and add the next white one — skip another white key and add the next white one. You now have a chord made up of three tones. Play any other key, white or black, within the octave (a range of eight white keys). Play different keys with your chord and note how the "color" changes. Adding an extra tone to a chord changes its color and is almost like painting one color over another to create fleeting impressions. Impressionistic music often has successions of colored chords.

Harmony and Melody

Classic and Romantic harmony emphasized contrary motion. Contrary motion is motion of one or more voice parts moving in the opposite direction of one or more other voice-parts. For example if the soprano goes up, the bass moves down. Impressionists often had all voices moving in the same direction. This is called parallel motion if the voices are kept the same distance apart, otherwise it is called similar motion. A series of chords in parallel motion or similar motion in the whole-tone scale creates a feeling of atmosphere and vagueness.

Impressionistic melodies very often seem to avoid natural direction. Listen to a slow movement of a Classic or Romantic symphony. Note how easy it is to follow the melody and almost anticipate where it is going. Now play a number by an Impressionist and note how he creates a rather elusive melodic line by avoiding natural melodic contour.

LISTENING TECHNIQUES FOR IMPRESSIONISM

A composer is expected to have high artistic ideals and a certain amount of perfection in his work. Performing artists are expected to hold to the score and present it in an authentic, artistic fashion with great sensitivity. We, as listeners, must present ourselves in a receptive mood. Our mental attitude is a very important factor in our enjoyment or appreciation of music. This is especially true of Impressionism. Don't think or say, "This is not for me." Get rid of mental blocks.

There are many different kinds of Impressionistic music —

music for every mood or frame of mind. Quiet, imaginative Impressionistic music with its vagueness is obviously not the type of music to listen to after an exciting football game. This would not be giving the music a fair chance. Choose some time when all is calm; when you are at peace with the world, and you want to do a little daydreaming.

Impressionistic music is perhaps the most imaginative of all. As a listener, you must use your own imagination to a greater extent than with other types of music. The composer usually gives us a clue about the piece in the title but very few if any, program notes. Impressionism is very elusive and per sonal. Very few react in the same way toward any one compo- sition. There is so much that is indescribable with moods changing like clouds that have but fleeting moments of design and color.

We have all had the experience of watching clouds as they move slowly — change color — fade away. Listen to Debussy's "Clouds." His program note is but one sentence, "'Clouds' causes the appearance of the sky to change with the slow, sol- emn motion of the clouds, fading away into grey colors lightly tinged with white." The virtues of this piece are its vaguenes suspense and atmosphere.

There is a great variety in Impressionistic music. All in Impressionism is not quiet and calm as in Debussy's "Clouds. Listen to Respighi's "Pines of the Villa Borghese," the first one of the suite "Pines of Rome." Respighi gives us a musica picture of children at play in a public park where the pines ar old, tall and stately. In the midst of ancient surroundings the is plenty of noise as we may well expect — loud clashes — exci ment — all that goes with the experiences of normal children play.

The three main things to remember about listening to Im pressionistic music are: know the title or something about th piece; be receptive; give your imagination free reign. Some- times a great deal of pleasure may be had by guessing what t name of the piece may be and what the composer had in mind With some compositions it is quite possible to switch titles a make sense. It just means that you are looking at a subject from a different point of view. For instance the titles of Debussy's "Clouds" and "Festivals" could be exchanged. The clouds would become active as if before a storm and we woul have a view of the festival after all of the celebrants had de- parted.

Suggested Impressionistic Music:

The titles of Impressionistic music are an important clue to the contents. For this reason all of the subtitles in the various suites are given in this list.

Orchestral Compositions

Debussy: La Mer (The Sea), Three Orchestral Sketches.

1. From Dawn to Noon at Sea.
2. Frolic of the Waves.
3. Dialogue Between the Wind and the Sea.

Debussy: Nocturnes

1. Nuages (Clouds)
2. Fete (Festival)
3. Sirens (Sirens) (with women's voices)

Debussy: Prelude a l'apres-midi d'une faune
(Prelude to the Afternoon of a Faun)

Debussy: Printemps (Springtime — suite in two parts)

Delius: Over the Hills and Far Away

Delius: Summer Night on the River

Delius: On Hearing the First Cuckoo in Spring

Griffes: White Peacock (originally for piano)

Griffes: Clouds (originally for piano)

Griffes: Pleasure Dome of Kubla Kahn

Ravel: Rapsodie Espagnole

1. Prelude to the Night
2. Malaguena
3. Habanera
4. Fair

Ravel: Daphnis and Chloe, Ballet Suite No. 2

1. Daybreak
2. Pantomime
3. General Dance

Respighi: Fountains of Rome

1. The Fountain of the Valle Giulia at Dawn
2. The Triton Fountain at Morn
3. The Fountain of Trevi at Midday
4. The Villa Medici Fountain at Sunset

Respighi: The Pines of Rome

1. The Pines of the Villa Borghese
2. The Pines Near a Catacomb
3. The Pines of the Janiculum
4. The Pines of the Appian Way

Miscellaneous

Debussy: Piano Pieces —

Clair de lune (Moonlight)
Reflets dans l'eau (Reflections on the Water)
L'Isle Joyeuse (Isle of Joy)
Jardins sous la pluis (Gardens in the Rain)
Preludes
Poissons d'or (Goldfish)

Debussy: La Damoiselle Elue (Blessed Damsel) (Cantata for soprano, mezzo-soprano, women's chorus and orchestra)

Ravel: Gaspard de la Nuit (piano)

1. Ondine (Water-Sprite)
2. Le Gibet (Gallows)
3. Scarbo (Nocturnal-Imp)

Ravel: Introduction and Allegro (Chamber music for flute, clarinet, harp and string quartet)

Ravel: Tzigane (Violin solo with orchestra)

Ravel: Piano Concerto for Left Hand Alone (this could very well be classified as Neo-Classic)

Ravel: La Valse (for piano)

10
Post-Romanticism
(1890-1945)

CHARACTERISTICS

The Post-Romanticists are those composers who carried the banner of Romanticism from the late 19th century into the 20th century. Among those who may be classified as Post-Romanticists are: Serge Rachmaninoff, Gustav Mahler, Richard Strauss and Jean Sibelius. They were inclined to use very large orchestras and write long symphonic compositions. They placed great emphasis on the emotional qualities in music, developed greater tone color in orchestration and used more advanced 20th-century harmonic idioms than the earlier Romanticists. An idiom in music may be rather loosely defined as being a "language" or style of writing.

RACHMANINOFF, MAHLER, STRAUSS, SIBELIUS

Serge Rachmaninoff (1873-1943)

For a time in America the compositions of the Russian composer, Serge Rachmaninoff, were among the most popular of all that may be classified as Post-Romantic. As time goes on, most of them are falling by the wayside. However, the three mentioned in the suggested list on page 90 seem to be holding their own with audiences and still appear on programs.

They are perhaps the easiest listening of all listed here under Post-Romantic. They are full of lush harmonies and emotional melodies that are easy to follow. Whatever Rachmaninoff has to say in his music, he says with enthusiasm. The faster movements are exuberant and at times irresistible. For those who want music for sheer pleasure and music that is more enduring than the type that is written just for fun, we recommend Rachmaninoff's.

Gustav Mahler (1860-1911)

Gustav Mahler composed with profoundly deep emotional sincerity. He expanded the orchestra to enormous proportions and, in four of his ten symphonies (Nos. 2, 3, 4 and 8), he added vocal parts. He felt the need of words to help bear his musical message. His music was his mission in life — to him a tremendous responsibility. The texts that he chose seem so personal because they fit in with the philosophy of the man — one who was known for his constant anxiety about eternity.

Mahler's Second Symphony, "Resurrection," is scored for an enormous orchestra, pipe organ, soprano and alto soloists and mixed chorus. The fourth movement, "Eternal Light," is an alto solo. The fifth movement, "Resurrection," is about thirty minutes long but so varied with soprano and alto solos and duets, male chorus, mixed chorus and orchestra, that no one need be alarmed about the length. The entire symphony takes about one hour and fifteen minutes.

We suggest that you do not listen to the entire work at first. Start with the fourth movement. Get well acquainted with this, then get acquainted with the fifth movement. After you have put these two movements together, you will have your curiosity aroused about the first part of the symphony, and will be much more receptive to it. Your mental attitude is important — listen as if "you were there."

An acquaintance with Mahler's "Resurrection" Symphony can be very helpful to those who have difficulty "getting" the more difficult moderns. The emotional values in the vocal parts are more easily related to our own experiences. Between passages or sections that are easy listening, there are passages that are in more advanced melodic and harmonic idioms, or more in keeping with what one might expect of contemporary writing. You will be getting some advanced contemporary idioms in small doses and relief in the romantic idioms.

Mahler's "Das Lied von der Erde" is one of the greatest

song cycles ever written. It requires considerable study and listening for the average person but any one will be greatly rewarded for the effort. Both this and the "Resurrection" Symphony are marvelous pieces to bridge the gap between romantic and some contemporary trends. Mahler's idioms in his symphonies and song cycles are a combination of the past and the present.

For further listening suggestions for this symphony and the suggested song cycles of Mahler, see listening techniques for the art song and song cycle page 70 and page 73.

Richard Strauss (1864-1949)

The music of Richard Strauss is full of poignant emotional expression. The dissonances, once shocking, are now accepted as a natural means of expression. Only the most successful, popular favorites are in the suggested list.

The two symphonic tone poems, "Death and Transfiguration" and "A Hero's Life," are not only among the composer's most successful and best works, but are rather accessible listening. A listener must constantly increase his capacity to listen to longer works. These two tone poems are excellent ones with which to increase one's capacity to "stay" with the music because they are imaginative, full of interesting subject matter, and are psychologically well constructed. See Symphonic Tone Poem, page 55.

The "Burlesque" for piano solo and orchestra, written when the composer was twenty-one, is growing in popularity. This brilliant work is full of lively, sparkling, happy music. Don't miss it.

The opera, "Der Rosenkavalier," is a very popular and successful one. It is by far the easiest listening of all the Strauss operas.

Jean Sibelius (1865-1957)

The Finnish nationalist composer, Jean Sibelius, has been loved the world over for his "Finlandia," an expression of patriotic fervor unequaled in all symphonic literature. His music is Scandinavian, very different from the other three Post-Romanticists mentioned. Sibelius' symphonic literature is quite varied — brooding, mystical, spiritual, patriotic, folklike, plaintive, robust — the full gamut of the emotions are to be found in his music with its indescribable Nordic flavor.

Sibelius has been a patriot of the first order — loving his native Finland with its steeply rolling countryside, its forests and its lakes. The patriot is heard in "Finlandia" — the north country and its legends are reflected in "The Swan of Tuonela." These are excellent prerequisites for Sibelius' symphonies. The "Second Symphony" is a good one to start with.

Suggested Post-Romantic Music:

Symphonies —

Mahler: Symphony No. 1 in D, "Titan"

Mahler: Symphony No. 2 in c minor, "Resurrection"

Rachmaninoff: Symphony No. 2, Op. 27

Sibelius: Symphony No. 2 in D, Op. 43

Sibelius: Symphony No. 4, Op. 63

Sibelius: Symphony No. 5, Op. 82

Tone Poems —

Sibelius: Finlandia, Op. 26, No. 7

Sibelius: Swan of Tuonela

Strauss: Till Eulenspiegel's Merry Pranks, Op. 28

Strauss: Tod and Verklarung (Death and Transfiguration), Op. 24

Strauss: Ein Heldenleben (A Hero's Life), Op. 40

Solo Instruments with Orchestra —

Rachmaninoff: Rhapsody on a Theme of Paganini for Piano and Orchestra, Op. 43

Rachmaninoff: Concerto No. 2 for Piano and Orchestra, Op. 18

Sibelius: Concerto in d minor for Violin and Orchestra, Op. 47

Strauss: Burlesque in d minor for Piano and Orchestra

Opera —

Strauss: Der Rosenkavalier

Art Songs —

Mahler: Ich bin der welt abhanden gekommen
(I am lost to the world)

Mahler: Ich atmet einen linden duft (I breath a gentle
scent)

Mahler: Um mitternacht (At midnight)

Song Cycles —

Mahler: Kindertotenlieder (words by Friedrich Ruckert)

1. Once more the sun would gild the morn
2. Ah, Now I know why oft I caught you gazing
3. When my mother dear
4. I think oft they've only gone abroad
5. In such a tempest

Mahler: Das Lied von der Erde (The Song of the Earth)

(8th-century Chinese texts)

1. The Drinking Song of Earthly Woe (tenor solo)
2. The Lonely One in Autumn (contralto solo)
3. Of Youth (tenor solo)
4. Of Beauty (contralto solo)
5. The Drunken One in Spring (tenor solo)
6. (a) Awaiting a Friend (contralto solo)
   (b) The Farewell of a Friend (contralto solo)

11
Other Twentieth-Century Developments

WHAT IS MODERN MUSIC?

The average person seems to think that compositions with dissonance are "modern" and that all "modern" music is dissonant. This is a misunderstanding that places contemporary music at a disadvantage. Dissonance in various degrees may be found in music of all ages. Palestrina, Bach, Haydn, Mozart Beethoven, Tchaikovsky, Chopin and all the other "favorite" composers of the general public have dissonances in their compositions.

Many are reluctant to give new music a fair trial. This attitude is not new. Debussy's "Prelude to the Afternoon of a Faun" was loved and hated when it was first performed and Stravinsky's "Rite of Spring" was called outrageous. Today both are approved by audiences all over the world.

Many of Beethoven's first performances were failures, partly because his manuscript was so poorly written that it wa difficult to read. The musicians were not very well trained an certainly the theatre lighting must have been next to impossib by our present-day standards.

Today the difficulties that confronted Beethoven do not exist. Stravinsky's manuscript is as neat and exact as printed music. The performers are the finest in history and the lighting is excellent.

Where does the difficulty lie in the failure of a contemporary work that shows up later as a great success? Primarily with the listener; he has a greater responsibility than he realizes. In the first place he must have the proper mental attitude. He must be tolerant and listen to some contemporary works many times before he arrives at a fair evaluation of them in relation to his listening pleasure and development. Some are not easy to become familiar with and only with familiarity can we expect to comprehend, appreciate or enjoy new music.

A sympathetic understanding of the literary content of contemporary program music is also very important. Let us consider parts of Samuel Barber's "Medea," the ballet music supporting the scenes depicting some of the episodes of the Greek legend.

Greek mythology tells of Medea, one of the most fiendish characters ever conceived by the imagination of man. She killed her two sons because she was angry with their father, Jason. Can you imagine Barber depicting this scene with a sweet, singable, sentimental melody?

Composers, critics and analysts are also partly to blame for widening the gap between the music and the average listener because they often present a scholarly analysis of the music in such a way that only they themselves can understand it. Furthermore they come out with a lot of "isms" in describing the music. They use terms such as futurism, neo-primitivism, neo-mysticism, proletarianism, pseudo-exoticism, utilitarianism, etc. until the average person is so confused and discouraged that he is inclined to give up in despair.

Don't let all this stop you from exploring contemporary music. If you are not up to Expressionistic music, the most difficult of all listening, there are many other kinds of music being written today. There are 20th-century compositions that have all of the characteristics of Romantic music, some have qualities of Impressionism, some have traces of Baroque or Classic ideas, still others have a very strong popular idiom. In other words there is no such thing as a definite type of music that can be called "modern."

Explore new fields of listening occasionally. Your taste changes from time to time. Composers are always looking ahead, exploring new possibilities. They all hope that their music will enjoy successful hearings. The composer is writing for you as well as for himself.

Rarely do we find imitators whose works are as great as those of the innovators. Should we be old-fashioned and rest

in the arms of the arts of our grandmothers? Writing a classi
minuet is about as absurd as going back to living in a log cabin

We would like also to direct the reader's attention to the
discussion of Neo-Classicism. Neo-Classic music is very ap-
proachable and is one phase of contemporary developments
that is very heartening to the less experienced listener who
finds Expressionism too difficult.

The miscellaneous list of 20th-century music is given with
comments to show the infinite variety of music of our times.
In this list you will find some musical craftsmanship, some
experimentation, some objectivity, some emotional restraint,
some emotional emphasis and endless types and kinds of music
The characteristics of Romanticism that so many people like
are to be found in the works of many composers.

Be an explorer. There are endless hours of pleasure wait
ing for those who have the right attitude and are willing to take
a chance.

EXPRESSIONISM

The music of the Expressionists, Arnold Schönberg (1874-
1951), Alban Berg (1885-1935) and Anton Webern (1883-1945),
is not for the average listener. It is the most difficult of all
listening but even though you may not care for it, a knowledge
of some of the phases of this development will aid in understanding many other contemporary compositions that have
traces of Expressionism.

Only musicians and the most rugged explorers are sturdy
enough to listen to very much Expressionism. It has been quit
aptly defined as "cerebral" music. If you are one of the rugge
or curious, we hope that the following information and suggestions will be helpful.

Expressionism in music is a radical departure from all
traditional standards. It is full of new experiences for those
who have heard only the conventional. The melodic lines, with
their odd and long skips, are not "natural," the harmonies are
often clear uncushioned dissonances, and the rhythms are ofte
complex and changing within the composition.

The term "Expressionism" is a very misleading one. In
the arts it does not mean emotional expression but rather the
personal expression of the composer — the inner self. If the

prefix "im" in Impressionism means impressions of the outer world, the prefix "ex" in Expressionism indicates expression of the subconscious inner self of the composer.

Atonality and the Twelve-Tone Techniques

Many creative artists forge ahead exploring new fields. Sometimes the composer finds new fields of expression within certain scales or families of tones, called "keys." When traditional keys do not serve his purpose he explores the possibilities of new ones. This is exactly what Schönberg did.

Let us review briefly what has happened to keys or families of tones through the centuries and the type of music that we associate with each development. Looking back, we think of each phase as being perfectly normal and acceptable, but when they were first presented or introduced, some of them were not accepted any more favorably than some of Schönberg's ideas are by many today.

Through the years the pitches within the octave have been changed and different order and arrangement of tones within the octave have been introduced. The Gregorian Chant was sung in an untempered or so-called "natural" scale; the church music of Palestrina was sung in a "mean-tone" system of tuning; and, although it may be traced back to 1518, the equal-tempered scale was not in practical use until during the Baroque period. The temperament for Bach's "Well-Tempered Clavier" (1722) was probably only approximate. During the Baroque period, major and minor keys were established; a great preparation for Haydn and Mozart who explored refinement in the Classic style.

After the Classicists came the Romanticists who explored the emotional possibilities of the major and minor keys. It is interesting to note that present-day temperament of the scale was not adopted throughout all Germany until about 1800, the beginning of the Romantic period; and not in England and France until about 1850, the middle of the Romantic period.

In the latter part of the 19th century, the Impressionist, Debussy, revolted against emotional Romanticism. He explored the possibilities of the whole-tone scale and showed preference for it for purposes of vagueness and atmosphere. At that time Debussy's music was treated with scorn by many, but today we enjoy it and accept it whole-heartedly.

In the early part of the 20th century, Schönberg explored the possibilities of still another family of tones, or tonality. By using all twelve tones within the octave, he developed a new kind of music commonly called "atonal," which literally means "no key." From the composer's point of view, it is a "twelve-tone technique" or "method of composing with twelve tones." At the piano for instance, it merely means that you use all the keys, both black and white, and one pitch is just as important as any other. This makes the music sound as if the composer destroyed "home base" and is one reason for the strangeness in Expressionistic melodies.

The "twelve-tone technique," devised by Schönberg, is a system whereby a composer uses all of the twelve pitches within the octave and arranges them in some arbitrary order and uses this established unalterable order of pitches as the basis and source of material for an entire composition. This pattern is called a "tone-row" or "series" — the composition is called "serial music." The rhythm or length of the notes may be changed, the various pitches in the sequence may appear an octave higher or lower than their original position, the series may be inverted or played backwards (retrograde) and the retrograde form may be altered as mentioned before or any altered form may be transposed to any step of the chromatic scale. Discussion of many other possible changes and developments is too technical and not practical here. Composers will find endless possibilities with this system. Compare the above with the findings of the British Change Ringer. With twelve bells it is estimated that it would take thirty-seven years, three hundred and fifty-five days to play a total of near five hundred million different changes or patterns.

The unusual tonality, odd skips and wild leaps in this type of music make it difficult to follow and remember. The listener must expect to hear any serial music many times in order to get acquainted with it.

Polytonality

Expressionists sometimes composed with polytonality. This means that two or more tonalities are used simultaneous like playing the piano with one hand in one key, and the other

hand in another key. The harmonic structure is usually rather
thin, avoiding lush tone colors, so that all the melodic lines
are clear.

Mixed Rhythms — Polyrhythm — Difficult Rhythms

Expressionists, like many other contemporary composers,
use many different rhythms in one composition. When these
changes are rather frequent, it is called mixed rhythms. Sometimes the rhythms change very rapidly from one to another.

Polyrhythm, the simultaneous use of two different rhythms,
is also a common present-day practice. To illustrate polyrhythm, let us just suppose that in a single composition we
have march rhythm and waltz rhythm going on at the same
time. March rhythm, with four beats to a measure, and waltz
rhythm, with three beats to a measure, played simultaneously
might be counted out and appear as in the pattern below. The
accent or emphasis is placed on the first beat of each measure.
Note that the common denominator "12" is illustrated by the
vertical marks.

```
March 1 2 3 4 1 2 3 4 1 2 3 4 1 2 3 4 1
      |||||||||||||||||||||||||||||||||||||||||||||||||
Waltz 1 2 3   1 2 3   1 2 3   1 2 3   1
```

Some Expressionists and other contemporary composers
use rather difficult rhythms. It is much easier to follow music
if it has a "regular" beat. The average listener may or may
not be aware of it, but if he can tap his foot to the music, physi-
cally or mentally, it seems to hold together better. Try tapping
your foot to a waltz with accents at the beginning of each measure — ONE, two, three — ONE, two, three, etc. Now try a more
difficult rhythm in the same way — five beats to a measure or
seven beats to a measure. These are more difficult and certainly not as natural as the waltz with its three beats to a
measure.

In brief, Expressionistic music has some or all of the
following characteristics:

1. Atonality
2. Polytonality
3. Polyrhythm
4. Mixed Rhythms

LISTENING TO EXPRESSIONISTIC MUSIC

Expressionistic music in the twelve-tone technique is thought of as music for the intellect — more or less mathematical, without regard for human emotion. A composition intellectually conceived, full of complexities that are rather abstract, will, quite naturally, be baffling to the average listener. However, the author has found, in his class of hundreds of students who know little about music, that about 4 per cent of the untrained listeners show keen interest in Expressionism.

When melodies are difficult to remember it delays enjoyment. You must give these melodies more attention, and remember that one or two hearings are just not enough! We have a great advantage in recordings, being able to hear them over and over again by ourselves or with someone who is interested in trying to "get" the music.

When one of Gustav Mahler's symphonies was performed for the first time, he conducted the entire work, then sat down in the audience while another conductor took over and repeated it. New compositions might have a better chance if this sort of thing were done more often.

Avoid absolute music at first — start with program music. You will probably be a little more receptive, trying to get the composer's point of view through his program. Remember that Expressionistic music is primarily the expression of the composer's subconscious self.

Schönberg's "Verklarte Nacht" (Transfigured Night) is not Expressionistic: It is very dramatic and emotional — definitely a Romantic composition. He wrote it in 1899 and arranged it for string orchestra in 1917. It was first used as the score for Anthony Tudor's ballet "Pillar of Fire" in 1942.

Schönberg's exploration of the atonal or twelve-tone technique started about 1907. His "Five Pieces for Orchestra," written in 1909, is a suite of program pieces. One of them, "Summer Morning by a Lake," shows traces of Impressionism. The dissonances in this suite are vigorous, meaningful and not very difficult to comprehend. The melodic lines and the general atmosphere of the pieces are interesting and stimulating.

If, after listening to "Five Pieces for Orchestra," you are ready for more, we suggest trying Schönberg's concertos in the suggested list.

Alban Berg was one of Schönberg's pupils. His "Violin

Concerto" is one of the finest compositions ever written in the twelve-tone system. It is in two movements, the first a description of a girl friend, the second, a requiem for her. Berg was so grieved over the death and personal loss of this very dear friend that he seemed to want to create in this concerto something to perpetuate her memory. He used parts of Bach's "Est ist genug" (It is enough), from Cantata No. 60, "O Ewigkeit, du Donnerwort" in the second movement, which is especially moving. It is not easy listening for the beginner but greatly rewarding to the sturdy individual who has patience enough to listen to the work several times.

Suggested Expressionistic Music:

Berg: Concerto for Violin and Orchestra

Berg: Wozzeck (Opera) (For the more experienced listener)

Schönberg: Beleitungsmusik zu einer Lichtspielscene, Op. 34 (Accompaniment to a cinematographic scene) Not intended to be in connection with any actual film but rather an imaginary one.

Schönberg: Verklarte Nacht, Op. 4 (Romantic — not Expressionistic) (For Strings)

Schönberg: Concerto for Violin and Orchestra, Op. 36 (1936) (Difficult listening)

Schönberg: Concerto for Piano and Orchestra, Op. 42 (1943) (Difficult listening)

Schönberg: Five Pieces for Orchestra, Op. 16 (1909)

1. Premonitions, 2. Yesteryears, 3. Summer Morning by a Lake — colors, 4. Peripeteia (sudden reversal in dramatic action), 5. The Obbligato Recitative

Webern: Six Pieces for Orchestra, Op. 6
This is an interesting and unusual suite of unnamed pieces in different moods. As Expressionistic music goes, it is rather accessible for absolute music.

NEO-CLASSICISM

Neo-Classicism is a contemporary style of composing which is a return to the 18th-century classic point of view as far as clarity, balance of form and transparency of orchestration are concerned. It is a departure from the Classic style of writing in that the melodies and general presentation are in 20th-century idioms.

Clarity, balance of form and transparency of orchestration are characteristics that tend to make the Classic and Neo-Classic music easier to listen to and enjoy.

The various compositions in the suggested list are primarily Neo-Classic. In them you may find traces of Romanticism, Expressionism, etc., and it is also true that you may find traces of Neo-Classicism in many other contemporary compositions. There are also those compositions that are a mixture of different "isms" and defy classification.

Suggested Neo-Classic Music:

Britten, Benjamin (1913-   )

Ceremony of Carols — (Women's Chorus, Harp Accompaniment)

This is a very beautiful accessible choral work.

Four Sea Pieces, from the opera, "Peter Grimes"

1. Dawn, 2. Sunday Morning, 3. Moonlight, 4. Storm

Young Person's Guide to the Orchestra (with narrator)

Designed to assist the listener in getting acquainted with the instruments of the orchestra.

Hindemith, Paul (1895-   )

Theme and Four Variations "Four Temperaments" (for piano and strings)

Theme — Melancholic — Sanguine — Phlegmatic — Choleric. This is an excellent portrayal of the "Temperaments" in the composer's style in 1940.

Symphonic Metamorphosis on Themes by Weber (1943)

1. Allegro, 2. Turandot, Scherzo (from incidental music for the German version of a Chinese play), 3. Andantino, 4. March.

This is one of Hindemith's most popular works. It is enjoyed greatly by musician and nonmusician alike.

rokofiev, Serge (1891-1953)

Prokofiev's music is full of variety. It is a sort of mix-re of Classic clarity, Romantic emotion and contemporary lioms and flavor. It is strongly recommended to those who ave trouble in "getting" the more dissonant moderns.

Alexander Nevsky, Op. 78 (Cantata from incidental music)

This is for those who like bold, stirring, vocal and orchestral music. The setting of the historical film, for which the music was originally written, is dated 1242. This is an excellent example of music for films. In listening to this work, one should imagine himself a part of this 13th-century drama.

Classical Symphony in D, Op. 25 (for fun)

This is sophisticated satire on Classicism. Among other things we notice that Prokofiev did not include the traditional minuet for the third movement but in its place — a gavotte!

Symphony No. 7, Op. 131

This is obviously a "Romantic-Modern" — much tone color in orchestration — changing moods. The second movement is exhilarating and the fourth is irresistible.

Stone Flower (ballet)

Pleasant, easy listening — one to enjoy without much effort.

Piano Concerto, No. 3, Op. 26

Prokofiev made his reputation on this concerto. It is still recognized as one of his best works.

Piano Sonatas (9)

> Numbers one and two are good starters. If you have not heard these you have a treat in store. Traces of Impressionism may be found in Sonata No. 2.

Shostakovitch, Dmitri (1906-   )

First Ballet Suite

> This humorously ridicules Romantic European composers. It is delightful listening even if you find the humorous side a little too sophisticated. It is writte in a rather Romantic style.

Concerto for Piano and Orchestra, Op. 35 (1933)

> String orchestra with trumpet makes a very effectiv accompaniment for the piano. Truly Shostakovitch i style, with flavors of popular idioms.

Concerto for Piano and Orchestra, No. 2, Op. 101 (1957)

> This is not a profound work. Jolly themes and exciting rhythmic patterns in the first movement are followed by the beautiful stately romantic melodies of the Andante. The third movement has delightful rhythmic and technical fireworks. This concerto is very easy listening yet wears well.

Symphony No. 5, Op. 47 (1937)

> One of the most popular of the Shostakovitch symphonies. An excellent one to start with.

Symphony No. 10, Op. 93

> This beautiful symphony has many changing moods, plaintive melodies, brooding themes, stirring climax beautiful harmonies and exciting rhythms. It is an e ample of the mature Shostakovitch at his best.

Stravinsky, Igor (1882-   )

Firebird Suite (from the Ballet, 1910)

Petrouchka (Ballet, 1910)

Both of these ballets are well within reach of those who have had some experience with 20th-century music that is "different."

Symphony of Psalms (1930)

If you are a Stravinsky and choral enthusiast, you will enjoy this work with its texts from the Psalms. The double fugue may be a little difficult for the beginner but the last part, Psalm 150, is a thrilling reward.

Sacre du Printemps (The Rite of Spring) (1913)

Only for the rugged explorer.

Miscellaneous Twentieth-Century Music:

Bartok, Bela (1881-1945)

A musical craftsman of the first order, Bartok's imagination seems to be without bounds. He did more to explore the musical possibilities of percussion instruments than any other composer. His later works are more easily assimilated than his earlier compositions.

Concerto No. 3 in e minor, for Piano and Orchestra (1945)

This concerto, Bartok's last composition, is a masterful conclusion to a very productive life. It has in it many musical ideas that are typical of the composer throughout his career. Free and varied rhythms in the first and last movements with expressive melodies in the second are all created in quite traditional form. This is an outstanding contribution to 20th-century music.

Divertimento for String Orchestra (1939)

This spirited and sparkling composition is the most genial of all the numbers listed here.

Music for Stringed Instruments, Percussion and Celesta (1935)

Andante tranquillo, Allegro, Adagio, Allegro.

This suite is Bartok's greatest orchestral work. It

varies from subtle sombre moods to the most thrillin
rhythmic effects.

Sonata for 2 Pianos and Percussion (1937)

This is an exciting adventure for those who are looki
for "something unusual."

Bloch, Ernest (1880-1959)

Israel Symphony (1912-1916)

This program symphony is in three sections: Adagio
molto ("Prayer in the Desert"), Allegro agitato ("Yo
Kippur"), Moderato ("Succoth"). The symphony, star
ing and ending with prayerlike plaintive passages, is
neither "modern" nor "old-fashioned." In the last
movement two sopranos, two altos and a bass, placec
among the instruments of the orchestra, sing the
deeply moving strains, "In Thee I trust" and "Thou
art my refuge."

Sacred Service

This is a Jewish choral service — a masterpiece. Ar
other work of the composer that is not intended to be
"modern." However, it does have changing rhythms.
unusual melodic lines and 20th-century harmonic sty
but all blended in with traditional presentation of the
text. It is more difficult listening than the "Israel
Symphony."

Schelomo — Rhapsody for Violoncello and Orchestra (191

This is one of the most widely played and best knowr
of the works of Bloch. Hebraic melodies of varying
moods are fluently fashioned, one after the other.
Accessible at first hearing.

Chavez, Carlos (1899-   )

Toccata for Percussion (1942)

One of the most exciting pieces written for percussi
alone.

Dohnanyi, Ernst von (1877-1960)

Variations on a Nursery Theme (1913) (Piano solo and Orchestra)

The composer's most popular work. It is a series of witty variations in Romantic style, on a tune to which many, in years past, learned the alphabet.

Enesco, George (1881-1955)

Roumanian Rhapsody No. 1 (1907)

A popular piece which is made up of various Roumanian melodies, ranging from sentimental to bold and boisterous.

Falla, Manuel de (1876-1946)

Amor Brujo, El (Love, the Magician) (1915) (Ballet)

1. Introduction and Scene, 2. The Gypsies — Evening, 3. Scene of Sorrowing Love (with vocal solo), 4. The Homecomer, 5. Dance of Terror, 6. The Magic Circle, 7. Ritual Fire Dance, 8. Scene, 9. Song of the Will-o'-the-Wisp (with vocal solo), 10. Pantomime, 11. Dance of the Game of Love (with vocal solo), 12. Morning Chimes.

This is superb Spanish music with French Impressionistic influence. It is a pantomime ballet, but with vocal solos sung off-stage. Sometimes, in the orchestral suite, the numbers containing vocal parts are left out, or the voice parts are taken by instruments in the orchestra.

Nights in the Gardens of Spain (1909-1915)

1. In the Gardens of the Generalife, 2. Far-off Dance is Heard, 3. In the Gardens of the Sierra de Cordoba.

This suite is called "Symphonic Impressions, for Piano and Orchestra." The piano has a very important part in the orchestration but is not a solo instrument as in a concerto. The "Gardens of the Generalife" are gardens near the Alhambra. In the last number you hear a party in progress in the distance, with gypsies playing, dancing and singing. The whole suite is very festive.

Holst, Gustav (1874-1934)

The Planets, Op. 32 (1914-1917)

1. Mars, the Bringer of War, 2. Venus, the Bringer of Peace, 3. Mercury, the Winged Messenger, 4. Jupiter, the Bringer of Jollity, 5. Saturn, the Bringer of Old Age, 6. Uranus, the Magician, 7. Neptune, the Mystic.

This Romantic suite is written for a very large orchestra with large wind and percussion sections. Every instrument has an important part somewhere in the suite. A women's choir chanting a wordless chorus appears in the Impressionistic "Neptune." The subtitles are a guide for the general character of each number — moods ranging from poetic mysticism to very dramatic and powerful grandiose expression. There is a great wealth of orchestral tone color in these musical characterizations.

Ibert, Jacques (1890-   )

Divertissement for Chamber Orchestra

Introduction, Cortege, Nocturne, Valse, Parade, Finale.

This is a suite taken from Ibert's incidental music for "Le Chapeau de paille d'Italie." It was written for fun and is witty, irrestible, refined, musical humor. No thinking — just relax and listen!

Escales (Ports of Call) (1922)

Elusive musical impression of three Mediterranean ports of call — Palermo, Tunis and Valencia — developed out of three tunes heard on a voyage. The music is a lush combination of Impressionism and Romanticism.

Khachaturian, Aram (1903-   )

Concerto for Piano and Orchestra (1936)

> This brilliant popular work has considerable exotic
> flavor. The second movement is rather melancholy
> and a contrast to the gymnastic third movement, which
> sweeps on to a grand theatrical conclusion.

Gayne, Ballet Suite No. 1

> 1. Sabre Dance, 2. Dance of Ayshe, 3. Dance of the
> Rose Maidens, 4. Dance of the Kurds, 5. Lullaby,
> 6. Dance of the Young Kurds, 7. Armen's Variations,
> 8. Lezghinka.

Kodaly, Zoltan (1882-   )

Hary Janos Suite (1926)

> 1. Prelude. The Fairy Tale Begins, 2. Viennese
> Musical Clock, 3. Song, 4. The Battle and Defeat of
> Napoleon, 5. Intermezzo, 6. Entrance of the Em-
> peror and His Court.

> This descriptive suite from the comic opera, "Hary
> Janos," is an example of Hungarian nationalistic
> music. The "Intermezzo" is a czardas, a traditional
> Hungarian folk dance. The hero, Hary Janos, is a
> vain braggart of the first order, who claims he de-
> feated Napoleon single-handed.

Milhaud, Darius (1892-   )

Le Boeuf sur le Toit ("The Bull on the Roof" or
"Nothing Doing Bar")

> The music for this absurdly comical pantomime
> ballet was written in 1919 and based on Brazilian
> folk music. Listen to this for the fun of it — a lot
> of catchy tunes.

Le Creation du Monde (1923) (Ballet)

> This is the first piece of serious music to be written
> in jazz idioms. The ballet, with its Negro settings,
> was first performed in Paris by a Swedish Ballet!

107

If you want to see what jazz idioms were like in the "twenties," get this one.

Scaramouche Suite for Two Pianos

This is a perennially popular favorite with two-piano teams and audiences alike — the irresistible encore type. It was inspired by the composer's Brazilian experiences.

The Four Seasons

"Spring," dated 1935, is scored for violin and chamber orchestra. "Summer," dated 1951, is scored for solo viola, flute, oboe, clarinet, bassoon, horn, trumpet, two cellos and bass-viol. "Autumn," dated 1951, is scored for two pianos, flute, oboe, three horns, two violins and cello. "Winter," dated 1953, is scored for solo trombone and string orchestra. Although composed over a period of eighteen years this suite has unusual unity in character and style. It is interesting to compare these pieces with "The Seasons" by the Baroque composer, Vivaldi, and "The Seasons" by Glazounov, a Romantic composer.

Poulenc, Francis (1899-   )

Mass in G (1937)

1. Kyrie, 2. Gloria, 3. Credo, 4. Sanctus, 5. Agnus Dei.

This mass is a beautiful choral work that lasts about twenty minutes. The composer has caught a devotional aspect in Neo-Renaissance style that is extraordinary. Highly recommended.

Concerto for Organ, Strings and Timpani (1939)

Accessible contemporary organ compositions are hard to find. Here is one of which the average listener with some experience with contemporary idioms, need not be afraid.

Vaughan Williams, Ralph (1872-1958)

Symphony No. 2, "London" (1914: revised 1920)

This symphony, in traditional four movements, was intended to be absolute music. It is so illustrative of London — its fog, the Thames, Westminster, Big Ben, the jolly cockney and the bustle of a busy day — that a pictorial program has been attached to it. An impression of a day in London starts with the early morning fog and mist, then the city's awakening, the activities of the day, the evening, and then the return to quiet — it is midnight.

Symphony No. 3, "Pastoral" (1922)

The "Pastoral" is a Romantic-Impressionistic musical picture of the English countryside — the serenity of the gently rolling hills — small wooded areas — winding roads — all at peace with the world.

Symphony No. 7, "Sinfonia Antartica" (First performed in 1953)

(Orchestra, superscriptions, soprano voice and wordless chorus) Prelude, Scherzo, Landscape, Intermezzo, Epilogue.

The superscriptions are from the pen of Shelley, Coleridge and Donne, an extract from Captain Scott's Diary, and a portion of Psalm 104.

This "Sinfonia" originated in Vaughan Williams' music for "Scott of the Antarctic," the film which deals with Robert Falcon Scott's fatal 1912 exploration of the mysteries of the great white wilderness of the Antarctic. The musical impression of the heroic struggle to conquer the wastelands of the polar regions is tremendously impressive.

This is one of the most powerful musical pictures ever portrayed. The orchestration is magnificent. The music abounds in haunting ethereal effects, sudden surprises, ominous sounds — and then ... terror! The explorers suddenly confront an impassable ice

fall! The futile struggle against the savagery of
nature in the blizzard is depicted with superb artistry.

Villa-Lobos, Heitor (1887-1959)

Bachianas Brasileiras No. 5

The "Bachianas" is an invention of Villa-Lobos. It is
a melodic and polyphonic composition in a form similar to what Johann Sebastian Bach might have written,
but different in that the melodies and general atmosphere are just what you would expect of Latin American music.

Choros, No. 4 and No. 7

The "Choros" is another musical form invented by
this Brazilian nationalist. In the "Choros" he brings
together the native Indian and the popular Brazilian
musical idioms.

Forest of the Amazon

This suite of very descriptive music for symphony
orchestra, chorus and soprano soloist was completed
during the last year of the composer's life. It is
made up of the following numbers — Deep in the Forest, Excitement Among the Indians, Nature's Dance,
Savage War Dance, Sails, On the Way to the Hunt,
Twilight Song, Indians in Search of the Girl, Head
Hunters, Blue Dusk, Love Song and Forest Fire.
This suite, a very fine finale to the composer's very
productive life, was taken from the incidental music
which he wrote earlier for the film production of
Hudson's "Green Mansions."

Weinberger, Jaromir (1896-   )

Schwanda: Polka and Fugue

This is an orchestral encore favorite that is often
used to end a concert with a "lift."

12

Music for Band
and Brass Ensembles

The small brass ensemble dates back to the days of the early Roman empire when groups of brass players were called upon to play fanfares and the like to call attention to some important announcement or event.

From the latter part of the Renaissance to the early Classic period considerable music for brass instruments and pipe organ was written for religious services. During the 17th century, music was written for brass ensembles to be played from towers. For example, the brass ensembles by Johann Pezel listed on page 113, were written for town musicians who played from the Rathaus tower in Leipzig, Germany. They played twice daily, at 10 A.M. and 6 P.M.

As far as major composers were concerned, there appears to have been little interest in wind ensembles during the Romantic period. However at the turn of the century we find that the concert band, through its high artistic accomplishments, has attracted the attention and interest of many outstanding composers both here and abroad.

The list of suggested music for band and brass ensembles includes many different styles of writing. For the most part all of the pieces will be found to be rather accessible except perhaps the ones by Harris and Hindemith.

111

Suggested Band Music:

Barber, Samuel* (1910-   )
    Commando March (1943)

Hanson, Howard* (1896-   )
    Chorale and Alleluia (1953)

Harris, Roy* (1898-   )
    Symphony for Band

Hindemith, Paul (1895-   )
    Symphony in B flat for Band

Holst, Gustav (1874-1934)
    Suite No. 1 in E flat, Op. 28a (1909)
        Chaconne, Intermezzo, March
    Suite No. 2 in F, Op. 28b (1911)
        March, Song Without Words, Song of the Blacksmith
        and Fantasia on "Dargason"

Mennin, Peter* (1923-   )
    Conzona for Band

Persichetti, Vincent* (1915-   )
    Psalm for Band

Reed, H. Owen* (1910-   )
    La Fiesta Mexicana (1956)
        Prelude, Mass, Festival

Stravinsky, Igor (1882-   )
    Symphonies of Wind Instruments (1920)

Thomson, Virgil* (1896-   )
    A Solemn Music (1949)

Vaughan Williams, Ralph (1872-1958)
    Folk Song Suite (1924)
        March — Seventeen Come Sunday, Intermezzo —
            My Bonny Boy,
        March — Folk Songs from Somerset
    Toccata Marziale

---

*American.

Suggested Music for Brass Ensembles:

Altenburg, Johann Ernst (1734-1801)
    Concerto for Seven Trumpets and Timpani

Bach, C. P. E. (1714-1788)
    March for Three Trumpets and Timpani (For the Ark)

Berezowsky, Nicolai (1900-1953)
    Brass Suite, Op. 24 (1939)

Buonamente, Giovanni Battista (died 1625)
    Sonata for Brass Ensemble

Dahl, Ingolf (1912-   )
    Music for Brass Instruments (1944)

Gabrieli, Giovanni (1557-1612)
    Canzon septimi toni No. 1 (Venice, 1597) for double
    brass choir

Hindemith, Paul (1895-   )
    Morgenmusik (1932)

Pezel, Johann (1639-1694)
    Sonatas for 5 Brass Instruments
    Suite — Intrada, Sarabande and Bal

Sanders, Robert* (1906-   )
    Quintet in B flat (1942)

---

*American.

13
Music Appreciation in the Home

MUSIC FOR CHILDREN

Never in history has any country spent so much money on music in secondary schools and colleges as we do in the United States today. Most of it is spent on participation which is only a starter on the road to appreciation.

Participation is one thing and appreciation is another. Th is as true in music as it is in all of the other time arts: dram ballet, movies, radio and television. The person who plays a horn is no more capable of enjoying piano music than the person who has never played a musical instrument.

In music, participation and listening may go along hand-in-hand, or they may be developed separately. The performer must do considerable listening but very often his listening becomes specialized in the line of his participating interests.

The place to start music appreciation is in the home. There is no "right way" to introduce a child to music as a listening art. One "system" may be advisable in one home and not in another. We hope that some of the following suggestion will be helpful.

Taking time for a little music does not need to be a chore because there are so many excellent recordings designed to acquaint children with the instruments of the orchestra, the structural form of the symphony, program music and many other first-rate musical productions. These are so well done that the entire family can enjoy them together.

A record player of quality is one of the first consideratio

114

This is quite important. You cannot expect a child to be happy with an old discarded portable record player very long. How is he going to be able to get acquainted with the sound of orchestral instruments unless he gets accustomed to their true tone color? How is he going to get the feeling that enjoying good music is a part of gracious living if he is pushed off into his own room to play old beaten-up records and hillbilly stuff? This has its place but also has its limitations.

For the small child, a little music in the evening is an excellent substitute for the good-night story. Music for the child at bedtime and music for mother and father afterwards does not need to disturb the child's sleeping habits. If this is routine, it may even get to the point where he requests music for a few minutes so that he may be able to go to sleep. Regular habits like this give him a sense of comfort and a feeling that all is normal — all is well.

Various children's recordings are designed for different age levels. These age levels are not infallible. It depends upon the amount of listening experience and the interest of both the child and the parent. For example, it is not impossible or unusual for a child of six or seven to be able to identify all of the instruments of the orchestra. This study must continue, however, or like all other forms of early education, the child will lose this ability.

Children love pictures along with their records and their listening. Choose fine children's records with good illustrations and acquaint the child with two arts at the same time.

There are very fine recordings of nursery rhymes and songs. Introduce the children's versions of symphonic tone poems, ballets, etc., from time to time. "Hansel and Gretel," "Sleeping Beauty," "Swan Lake," "Peer Gynt," "The Night Before Christmas," and many others are available. Record companies are aware of the importance of this feature and are constantly improving the quality of their output.

Listen to original versions of program music with your child during this picture stage. Start with a short tone poem. or part of a suite that you know very well. Tell the whole story about the music first and then have a "running" commentary along with the music so that the child will know what is going on. A little acting or impersonating won't hurt.

In painting word pictures of the music, the parent develops his own imagination along with the child's and a feeling of closer personal relationship is brought about. Present-day home life is apt to grow into activities for individual members of the family. Listening to music can be interesting and inspiring to all.

If music has been a part of family life, it can be a great source of entertainment for a child when he is confined because of illness. It is not wasted effort to have good music on the radio or record player when the children are playing on the floor or playing quietly at some game. You may not be aware of it but some of it will make a lasting impression.

The following tone poems and descriptive suites are good starters in the field of program music for the whole family. These tone poems, individual numbers in the suites and movements of the symphonies, are rather short. This is important because the child's listening span is very limited. Suites with variety are desirable because the change in tempo and mood refreshes the interest. The record covers will have complete stories of the tone poems and suites. It is up to the parent to be well acquainted with the music so that he may explain what is going on while listening.

For ideas about listening to symphonic tone poems, refer to Chapter 8, page 55. The starting ages mentioned in the suggested list vary with the amount of listening experience.

Suggested Tone Poems for Children: (start at age 8 to 12)

Dukas: Sorcerer's Apprentice

> The apprentice gets into trouble because he did not know the magic word to stop the broom from carrying water — the whole place got flooded!

Liadow: Baba Yaga

> The old witch flies through the air to her hut on the mountain top.

Saint-Saens: Dance Macabre

> Children love the xylophone imitating the rattle of bones – the oboe representing the rooster crowing at dawn — the skeletons scuttling back to their graves.

Carpenter: Adventures in a Perambulator (see page 124)

Grieg: Peer Gynt (see page 65)

116

Kodaly: Hary Janos (see page 107)

Mussorgsky: Pictures at an Exhibition (see page 58)

Prokofiev: Winter Holiday — Children's Suite

> There is much realism in this suite. For example, when the children's train leaves the station for the country, the orchestra makes sounds like a train. The titles will give you a general idea of the contents of the suite. They are: Departure, Winter Night, Waltz on the Ice, The Bonfire, Song of the Boys, Evening Around the Stove, March, The Return.

Tchaikovsky: Nutcracker Suite (see page 18)

> This is a ballet with a Christmas story about a little girl who received a nutcracker as a Christmas gift. In her dream the nutcracker turned into a fairy prince who escorted her to see the various things interpreted in the ballet.

Saint-Saens: Carnival of the Animals (see page 58)

> For family fun, get the version with poems about the animals by Ogden Nash. The suite was written as a bit of humor and Nash's poems are a captivating addition to the original.

Suggested Symphonies for Children: (start at age 7 to 10)

McDonald: Children's Symphony (see page 119)

Mozart, Leopold: Toy Symphony

> A short conventional symphony played by two violins, double-bass, piano and a lot of toys: drum, trumpet, rattle, quail, cuckoo and nightingale.

Suggested Symphonies for Children: (start at age 10 to 13 and up)

Haydn: Symphony No. 88, "Paris"

Haydn: Symphony No. 96, "The Miracle"

ACQUAINTING CHILDREN WITH THE
INSTRUMENTS OF THE ORCHESTRA

It can be very interesting and easy for children to learn to identify the instruments of the orchestra by their tone color. There are very fine compositions and recordings that have been made especially for this purpose. These vary in content and age level.

Often there is a desire to discuss the music during or immediately after the playing of a record. It is advantageous in such discussions to be acquainted with the tone color of the various instruments. Some get a great deal of satisfaction out of just being able to identify the instruments without any outside motivation.

As a record is being played, it is interesting to look for the picture of the instrument that you are listening to and note its position in the orchestra. Refer to the illustration of the orchestral instruments and seating chart, page 14.

Record Suggestions:

Britten, Benjamin: Young Person's Guide to the Orchestra (with narrator)

Gillis, Don: The Man Who Invented Music (with narrator) (age 7 to 12)

It is Grandpa's night to be baby sitter. To get Wendy to go to sleep, he invents a delightful yarn about how he invented music and all the instruments. Some of the instruments are played separately — others are played in groups. Children love it and want to hear it over and over again. This helps arouse interest in the instruments.

Prokofiev, Serge: Peter and the Wolf (with narrator) (ages 8 to 80)

In this story, different instruments represent people, animals and birds. The flute represents the bird, the clarinet — the cat, the oboe — the duck, the bassoon — the Grandpapa, etc. This composition is a great favorite among both young and old.

Wilder, Alec: A Child's Introduction to "The Orchestra" and
   All Its Instruments (age 10 and up)

   The lyrics are by Marshall Barer with musical direction
      by Mitchell Miller. This is a delightful and interest-
      ing presentation — the best educational record of its
      kind. Start this one at age 10 or younger, depending
      on the amount of previous listening experience. The
      whole family will enjoy it.

A CHILD'S VERSION OF THE SYMPHONY

Most children like to be treated as adults. What a joy for
them to discover that a symphony was written with traditional
tunes that they know. Moreover, this symphony has the same
plan that they would find in the works of the great masters —
music that mother and father listen to. The symphony is Harl
McDonald's "Children's Symphony." This is the way it appears
on a printed program.

   Children's Symphony . . . . McDonald

      Allegro moderato
      Andante patetico
      Allegro scherzando
      Allegro marziale

Except for the title it looks pretty grown-up. "Allegro
moderato" means moderately fast, "Andante patetico" means
slow and sad, "Allegro scherzando" means fast and playful,
"Allegro marziale" means fast like a military march. Each
movement is quite different from the others except the first
and last are somewhat alike in that they are both fast. The
fast movements have a slow tune in them and the slow movement has a fast tune in it. We don't get as tired listening when
the music changes speed once in a while.
   Sometimes we hear only a short bit of the tune. The bits
are called "fragments" — meaning little pieces. Notice how the
tunes are tossed around from one instrument to another. All
the strange things that happen to the tunes have big names like
"episode" and "development." An "episode" is just something
going on while we are getting ready for another time. The "development" occurs where the composer changes the tunes a little

and at times it seems as if the tunes were all cut up and mixed up. Sometimes it sounds as if one tune was talking to another tune.

The tunes or themes used in the Children's Symphony are: Allegro — (first movement) "London bridge is falling down" and "Baa, Baa, Black Sheep," Andante — (second movement) "Little Bo Peep" and "Oh, Dear what can the matter be?," Scherzo — (third movement) "Farmer in the Dell" and "Jingle Bells," Finale — (fourth movement) "Honey Bee" and "Snow is falling on my garden."

For further information refer to Chapter 7. After you are well acquainted with the general construction of this little symphony, compare it with Haydn's Symphony No. 96, "The Miracle or Haydn's Symphony No. 88, "The Paris." These symphonies are both very easy listening and are recommended works of absolute music for the child who is willing to try to break away from program music occasionally.

14
American Music

All kinds of music will be found among the compositions by Americans. Some composers write in a very romantic vein, paying quite a bit of attention to expressive melodies and good psychological form and are not afraid of being a bit old-fashioned. Others reach out into unexplored realms, new mediums, creating new types of listening. Great strides are being made in America, looking toward new horizons in all branches of musical endeavor.

There is much experimenting. This is always a part of creative activity but occasionally there is a tendency for a few listeners to be artificially carried away with something that they cannot understand so that they may bask in the presence of what appears to be the avant-garde. On the other hand there is the conservative listener who may be too much inclined to avoid the new.

Practically all internationally recognized American music dates from the turn of the century. Musically we are a very young country. The first American to receive European recognition was Edward MacDowell (1861-1908). Others followed slowly but at present there are hundreds of composers who are struggling to be heard.

American works occupy only from 4 to 5 per cent of the programs of most major orchestras and the general public seldom has a chance to get acquainted with a number before it is withdrawn from the repertoire. From the standpoint of the conductors, managers and committees responsible for financial maintenance of the orchestras, the performance of more new American works or lesser known works is a bit hazardous.

One of the best ways to get acquainted with American music is by listening to records. The list of suggested music is by no means complete but it is hoped that the variety will give the reader a few starters and stimulate his curiosity and interest in American music.

Some of these works may continue to be performed while others may be discarded sooner or later and the discarded ones may have some influence on music of the future. This is something with which the listener need not be concerned. We are rarely concerned about the future value of a present-day musical show. Just enjoy listening to the music!

In most American music we find that the basic elements have not been ignored by the composers. It takes fine sensitive creative ability of considerable stature to write original melodies containing substance, character and vitality. However there are those who hold that melody is not as important in some contemporary idioms as it was formerly. Emotion, ranging from flagrant to extremely subtle, is a part of the expressive quality in music but some think this is old-fashioned. For some composers, form is psychologically an essential part of music if it is to convey its message in full and yet not overdo an idea in driving home a point but some feel that content is much more important. With some, splashes of harmonic color or fragments of melody are effective and a part of their style but others hold that this only leads to chaos. To some, harmony is very important even to the point of conforming to the early traditional, but with some composers other elements become more important.

There is no attempt made here to arrive at any conclusions or make any predictions about American music. With but few exceptions there is no attempt made to classify the composers since they are, for the most part, ruggedly individualistic.

Composers who have come to this country as mature musicians are not listed here. Bartok, Bloch, Hindemith, Milhaud, Stravinsky, etc., will be found elsewhere in this book. Italian-born Menotti and German-born Foss are listed here because most of their education and musical experience has taken place in America and Varèse because all of his electronic experimenting has been done in this country.

Suggested American Music:

Barber, Samuel (1910-   )

Adagio for Strings (1936)

This is a beautiful short lyric piece in romantic style, arranged by the composer from the slow movement of his String Quartet, Op. 11.

Essay for Orchestra, No. 1 (1938)

This is melodic and singable like the "Adagio." The first and third parts are slow. The middle section is a scherzolike allegro. The whole piece is unquestionably romantic. Beautiful music for the conservative listener.

Medea (Ballet, "Cave of the Heart") (1946)

1. Parados, 2. Choros — Medea and Jason,
3. The Young Princess — Jason, 4. Choros,
5. Medea, 6. Kantikos agonias, 7. Exodus.

A fine musical characterization of Medea and Jason, and the general atmosphere surrounding the episode depicting uncontrollable jealousy, and the horror of Medea's revenge in cruel fiendish murder.

Sonata for Cello and Piano, Op. 6 (1932)

This sonata, in three movements, is a very enjoyable, romantic composition.

Symphony No. 1, Op. 9 (1936: revised 1942)

In one long movement, this symphony has changes from dramatic to lyric, always with freshness in a Post-Romantic style. The dissonant passages enhance the effectiveness of the lyric sections.

Vanessa (First performed at the Metropolitan, 1958)

This opera, in spite of its somewhat shallow plot, has been rather successful. The libretto was written by Menotti. The music is quite accessible melodically.

Bennett, Robert Russell (1894-   )

Armed Forces Suite

> This is about as American as you can get. Sounds of
> guns, arrows, Indian drums, frontier combo, familiar
> songs and tunes of the times, machine guns, bugle
> calls, service songs, effectively contribute to the gen-
> eral atmosphere of this review of history. Various
> parts are played by symphony orchestra, symphonic
> band and small combo. The numbers of the suite are:
> (1) 1776 "When in the course of human events," (2)
> 1812 "What so proudly we hailed," (3) 1836 "Hark to
> the Indian yell ring on the air!" (4) 1845 "Near Buena
> Vista's mountain chain, Hurrah! Hurrah! Hurrah!"
> (5) 1861-64 "That these honored dead shall not have
> died in vain," (6) 1898 "Remember the Main," (7) 1917-
> 18 "to make the world safe for democracy," (8) 1941-
> 45 "Blood, sweat, and tears."

Bernstein, Leonard (1918-   )

Fancy Free (1944) (Ballet)

> This very gay and animated suite is easy listening.
> It is cast in a mixture of contemporary popular idioms
> with considerable Latin-American accent.

Carpenter, John Alden (1876-1951)

Adventures in a Perambulator (1914)

> 1. En Voiture, 2. The Policeman, 3. The Hurdy-
> Gurdy, 4. The Lake, 5. Dogs, 6. Dreams.

> The obvious program is delightful. Realism, Impres-
> sionism and Romanticism make this suite pleasant,
> easy listening. The Hurdy-Gurdy man becomes a
> real character, dodging the policeman; the dogs are
> playful; the lake is Lake Michigan; and the adventure
> takes place in Lincoln Park, Chicago. This suite is
> recommended for children from nine to ninety.

Copland, Aaron (1900-   )

Billy the Kid (Ballet Suite) (1938)

124

The story is about the outlaw, Billy the Kid. Cowboy tunes, carefree rhythms and musical impressions of the wide open spaces remind us of the "gun totin'" pioneer days.

Salon Mexico, El (1936)

The composer has captured an excellent musical impression of Old Mexico. The spirited melodies and rhythms in Latin-American idioms are irresistible. Here is fifteen minutes of good entertainment.

Quiet City (1940)

This is an adaptation of the incidental music that Copland wrote for the play by the same name. Interesting solo parts by the trumpet and the English horn set the general mood of this rather brooding piece depicting loneliness in the city.

Foss, Lukas (1922-   )

Time Cycle (1957)

The texts of the four songs in this cycle are "We're Late" by W. H. Auden, "When The Bells Justle" by A. E. Housman, "From Franz Kafka's Diaries — January 16" and "O Man! Take Heed!" from Friedrich Nietzsche's "Thus Spake Zarathustra." Now tonal, now atonal, now the music is more important, now the words are more important, now accessible, now far out, now the music is composed, now it is improvised, now an orchestra, now a chamber ensemble, now in English, now in German ... reflections on life, death, solitude, eternity ... "the clocks do not synchronize" ...

Gershwin, George (1898-1937)

For the most part, the works of Gershwin need no introduction and his sprightly jazz idioms need no explanation. There is originality in style but a bit of the sameness in all of his works.

American in Paris (1928)

A musical picture of an American's impressions,

125

while taking a walk down the Champs-Elysée in Paris The moods change in this tone poem as we hear impressions of French taxicabs, cafés, a church, an attack of homesickness, the Charleston, gayer moods and then... well, let's make the most of it. This is Paris!

Concerto in F for Piano and Orchestra (1925)

Porgy and Bess (An American Folk Opera) (1935)

This, Gershwin's last major work, contains the popular songs, "Summertime," "I got plenty of nuttin'," "You is my woman now," and "My man's gone now."

Rhapsody in Blue (1924) (Piano and Orchestra)

Gillis, Don (1912-   )

Frontier Town (Ft. Worth, Texas — Descriptive Suite) (1940)

1. Chamber of Commerce (satirical take-off), 2. Where the West Begins (languid contentment), 3. Ranch House Party (gay, carefree — good time was had by all), 4. Prairie Sunset (colorful impressions), 5. Main Street — Saturday Night (humorous and boisterous). All are in a popular idiom.

The Man Who Invented Music (script by Claris Ross and Gillis) (1949)

A child's bedtime story and music that helps acquaint the listener with the instruments of the orchestra. (See page 118)

Symphony No. 5 1/2 (A Symphony for Fun) (1946-1947)

No introduction necessary — just follow the titles of the four traditional (?) movements. (a) Perpetual Emotion, (b) Spiritual?, (c) Scherzofrenia, (d) Conclusion!

Symphony No. 7 ("Saga of a Prairie School") (1948)

This was written for Texas Christian University, Fort Worth, Texas for their diamond jubilee celebration. The movements are: Vision, The People, The Dedication and The Fulfillment.

Gould, Morton (1913-   )

Spirituals for Orchestra (1942) (Suite in Jazz Idioms)

The captivating moods in the various numbers are consistent with their titles, which are Proclamation, Sermon, A Little Bit of Sin, Protest and Jubilee.

Latin-American Symphonette

The composer has captured Spanish musical flavor with exotic Caribbean, Negro and Indian influence in these delightful dances: 1. Rhumba, 2. Tango, 3. Guaracha, 4. Conga.

Griffes, Charles Tomlinson (1884-1920) (See pp. 81 and 85)

Grofe, Ferde (1892-   )

Grand Canyon Suite (1931)

1. Sunrise, 2. Painted Desert, 3. On the Trail, 4. Sunset, 5. Cloudburst.

This popular orchestral suite of tone poems abounds in Impressionism and Realism with considerable Romanticism to tie it together. "Sunrise" is especially beautiful as the colorful orchestration seems to unfold darkness into dawn and the glories of a new day. The stubborn donkey in "On the Trail" is a good bit of humorous realism. The thunder and lightning with the torrents of rain in "Cloudburst," are so real that you are practically prompted to put up your umbrella.

Hanson, Howard (1896-   )

Symphony No. 1, "Nordic" (1922)

This rather youthful work in three movements has somewhat of a program in that the composer wished to present in the first movement, a musical conception of his Nordic ancestors. The second movement, dedicated to his mother, is probably a musical portrait of her and the third movement, dedicated to his father,

127

is probably a portrait of him. This symphony is much
easier listening than some of the composer's later
works.

Symphony No. 2, "Romantic" (1930)

This symphony in three movements is well named,
for it is truly Romantic in every sense of the word.
The melodies are beautiful, singable tunes. The
entire symphony is very accessible.

Harris, Roy (1898-   )

Symphony No. 3 (1939)

This work is one of the few American compositions
that has continued in the repertoire of a few major
symphonies. It has appeal to both musician and
audience, is not very long, has accessible melodies
and is in one movement. Harris has furnished the
following program for the four sections of the symphony: Tragic, Lyric, Pastoral and Fugue.

Ives, Charles (1874-1954)

Three Places in New England (1903-1914)

Sometimes referred to as "A New England Symphony"
this suite has the following titles: The 'Saint Gauden
in Boston Common; Putnam's Camp, Redding, Conne
ticut; The Housatonic at Stockbridge. Ives' creative
genius is exemplified in these musical pictures. Re
peated listening and close study of these pieces will
open up a new world for the conscientious rugged
explorer. Only recent years have brought an appreciation of this composer. He was far ahead of his
time. The following lines are from a poem which is
a preface to the first picture:

"Moving — Marching — Faces of Souls!
 Marked with generations of pain,
 Part-freers of a Destiny,
 Slowly, restlessly — swaying us on with you
 Towards other Freedom! - - - - - -"

In the second musical picture we hear two bands each
marching toward the center of the town from opposite
directions, each band playing a different march. The
resultant clash of sound can hardly be imagined. The
third number is a musical setting of a New England
countryside, inspired by a walk through meadows
along the river near Stockbridge.

MacDowell, Edward (1861-1908)

Piano Concerto No. 2, Op. 23 (1885)

In true Romantic solo concerto style, this has plenty
of fireworks, melody and varying moods. The second
movement is fascinating and lively with considerable
syncopation — the popular rhythm of the day. This is
MacDowell at his best.

McBride, Robert (1911-   )

Mexican Rhapsody (1936)

Spirited, light-hearted "south of the border" music
introducing "Mexican Hat Dance," "La Cucaracha"
and "Allá en el Rancho Grande." Delightful entertainment.

Menotti, Gian-Carlo (1911-   ) (Italian-American)

Menotti's musical shows are all effective theatrical productions. The style is a fusion of Romantic, Impressionistic
and Contemporary idioms. "Amahl and the Night Visitors" is
best known and best loved of all. The tragedies are difficult
listening at first but the theatrical side is so tremendous that
they soon "get under your skin."

Amahl and the Night Visitors (TV Christmas Chamber
Opera) (1951)

Amelia Goes to the Ball (1937) (One Act Comic Opera)

The Consul (1950) (Musical drama — a tragedy in three acts)

The Medium (1946) (Musical drama — a tragedy in two acts)

The Old Maid and the Thief (1939) (Comic Opera originally
for radio — then for TV)

Mitchel, Lyndol (1923-   )

>Kentucky Mountain Portraits (1948-1956)

>>1. Cindy, 2. Ballad, 3. Chivaree. Program music in a very light popular vein, portraying varying moods from sentimental to raucous.

Moore, Douglas (1893-   )

>The Pageant of P. T. Barnum

>>This suite depicts the following episodes in the life of the celebrated showman: 1. Boyhood in Bethel, 2. Joice Heth, the 160-year-old Negress, 3. General and Mrs. Tom Thumb, famous midgets, 4. Jenny Lind, the incomparable coloratura soprano, 5. Circus Parade, depicting the calliope by the out-of-tune clarinet.

Phillips, Burrill (1907-   )

>Selections from McGuffey's Readers

>>A descriptive suite ranging from the jolly syncopated rhythms of "The One Horse Shay" with all the humor that is associated with it, to the tender and expressive "John Alden and Priscilla" and finally the mysterious and dramatic "Midnight Ride of Paul Revere."

Piston, Walter (1894-   )

>The Incredible Flutist (Suite from the Ballet)

>>The ballet music, originally written in 1933, had its premiere in 1938. In 1940 the suite, abridged by the composer himself, was first performed by the Pittsburgh Symphony Orchestra. It is divided into twelve episodes as follows: 1. Introduction, 2. Dance of the Vendors, 3. Entrance of the Customers, 4. Tan 5. Entry of the Circus, 6. Circus March, 7. Solo c the Flutist, 8. Minuet, 9. Spanish Waltz, 10. Eigh O'Clock, 11. Siciliano, 12. Polka Finale.

Taylor, Deems (1885-   )

>Through the Looking Glass

The full orchestral version of this humorous suite is dated 1922. It continues in the repertoire of some orchestras as a perennial favorite. The suite, named after Lewis Carroll's story by the same name, contains the following: 1a. Dedication, 1b. The Garden of Live Flowers, 2. Jabberwocky, 3. Looking-glass Insects, 4. The White Knight.

Thompson, Randall (1899-   )

Symphony No. 2 (1931)

A delightful, unforced, agreeable work in popular idioms reminiscent of the 1920's with unmistakable influence or experimentation with ragtime, syncopation and blues. The fast movements have delightful rhythms, the third movement having 7/4, 6/8 and 9/8 time. The Largo is lush and romantic with its melancholy blues typical of some of the popular music of the roaring twenties.

Thomson, Virgil (1896-   )

The following are fine examples of incidental music for films. The music is so pictorial in mood that it is easy for the listener to visualize the story for which the music was written.

Louisiana Story (1948)
Pastoral, Chorale, Passacaglia, Fugue.

The Plow that Broke the Plains (1936)
Prelude, Grass, Cattle Songs, Blues, Drought, Devastation.

Varèse, Edgar (1885-   )

Varèse is often referred to as one of the greatest experimenters in sound. He objects to having his work called "experimental" since, as he says, the experimenting has been done and now it is up to the listener to experiment. The following are listed for those who are interested in sound effects, unique musical thought and abstract experiences.

Density 21.5 (1936)

> This is a composition for unaccompanied flute. It was written for Georges Barrer and his platinum flute. Platinum has a density of 21.5.

Hyperprism (1924)

> This is written for an odd assortment of percussion instruments and a group of wind instruments. Most of the time, when both groups are playing together, they are playing in different rhythms.

Integrales (1926)

> Eleven wind instruments and seventeen percussion instruments join forces in this composition.

Ionisation (1931)

> This piece requires thirteen players. It is written for thirty-seven percussion instruments ranging from conventional to exotic. You have to hear it to believe it.

Octandre (1924)

> Written for piccolo, flute, clarinet, piccolo clarinet, oboe, bassoon, horn, trumpet, trombone and string bass. Unique musical material in conventional form.

Poeme Electronique (1958)

> This is perhaps the most unique of all the works of Varèse. It was designed to provide continuous sound for the Philips Radio Corporation's pavilion at the Brussels Exposition. It is interesting to get listeners reactions to this piece which employs electronic and percussive sounds with human voices added occasionally near the end. The results are often very weird and unearthly.

Glossary

This glossary is made up of terms used in this handbook, often used in general conversation about music and commonly found in program notes. It is not intended to be a complete music dictionary nor is it intended to deal with the terms except in their general usage in this book. Very often a term has different meanings depending upon (1) the period in music history with which it is associated, e.g., "sonata," (2) the commonplace or the learned usage, e.g., "classic," (3) the literary, scientific or musical meaning, e.g., "dynamic." All definitions have been simplified as much as possible so as to avoid confusion. For further and more detailed information we suggest that you refer to the latest edition of a reliable complete dictionary of music.

Absolute Music. Music in which the composer presents various moods that have no literary or pictorial program.

Aria. A song for solo voice that is a part of a major work such as an opera, oratorio or a cantata.

Art Song. A song of high artistic quality for solo voice. The text is usually a very fine lyric poem that is supported by or fused with a sympathetic accompaniment. The German Art Song or Lied made its appearance with Franz Schubert's lieder (pl.) in the early nineteenth century. These songs of Schubert are with piano accompaniment. Later some composers used an orchestral accompaniment, e.g., the Art Songs of Gustav Mahler. See pages 70 and 91.

Atonal. Literally without a key but more accurately applied to its general usage in referring to music composed by means of the "twelve-tone technique" or method of composing with all of the twelve tones within the octave. This is a great departure from the traditional classic and romantic approach. See page 95.

Ballet. An artistic theatrical dance, performed by a group of dancers in appropriate costumes, to the accompaniment of music. See page 62.

Baroque. A period in art history that dates quite definitely from 1600 to 1750. The music of the period is in general serious, with an abundance of polyphonic as well as homophonic literature in which the listener may expect well-defined melodies and regular rhythms. See Chapter 5, page 26.

Baroque Solo Concerto. A composition with considerable polyphonic treatment written for a solo instrument and orchestra. See page 30.

Baroque Suite. A group of antique dances. See page 29.

Cadenza. A section of a composition for solo voice or solo instrument that is written in free style giving the soloist a chance for considerable technical display. Compositions where cadenzas are most commonly found are the classic and romantic concertos and very often operatic arias, particularly those for soprano.

Cantata. A vocal work with either sacred or secular text for solo voice(s) and chorus, usually with orchestral accompaniment. See Bach cantatas, page 35.

Chamber Music. Generally thought of as music for a small group of instrumentalists that was originally intended to be performed for small audiences in rather intimate surroundings — not a *large* concert hall. See page 50.

Choir of the Orchestra. A body of instruments in the symphony orchestra having some common trait or characteristic such as the string choir, wood-wind choir, brass choir or percussion choir. See Chapter 2, page 13.

Chorale. A reformation term given to a hymn to be sung by the church congregation in the language of the people. See page 34.

Chorale Prelude. An organ composition based on the tune of a chorale. See page 34.

134

Classic. In ordinary and deteriorated usage the term classic
seems to be applied to any music that appears to be first-
rate. In this book the term is used in connection with the
Viennese Classicists, Haydn, Mozart and Beethoven. It
should be noted that the later works of Beethoven are more
romantic in character than those of either Haydn or Mozart.
For a more thorough discussion see Chapter 7, page 39.

Coda. A sort of conclusion or "epilogue" found at the end of a
composition such as in the sonata-allegro form. See
page 44.

Codetta. A semiending at the end of a section of a composition.

Color. Color in music is the psychological interpretation of
the quality of sound produced by any instrument(s), voice(s),
device(s) or any combination thereof. See (7) page 12.

Comic Opera. Same as Opéra Comique.

Concertino. The solo group in the Concerto Grosso. See
page 31.

Concerto. In general a composition for solo instrument and orchestra. With but few exceptions the classic construction
of the solo concerto, with its three movements (fast, slow,
fast) and cadenzas, has been retained since the time of
Mozart. See page 48.

Concerto Grosso. This type of concerto differs from the solo
concerto in that there is a group of solo instruments and
the entire orchestra. It should not be confused with concertos written for two solo instruments, such as Brahms'
"Concerto for Violin, 'Cello and Orchestra" which is called
a "double concerto," nor concertos written for three solo
instruments, such as Beethoven's "Concerto for Violin,
'Cello, Piano and Orchestra" which is called a "triple
concerto." See page 30.

Contrary Motion. One or more voices in the harmonic or polyphonic structure moving in the opposite direction to one or
more other voices.

Contrapuntal (adjective). In the style of counterpoint.

Counterpoint. Literally melody against melody. The simultaneous use of two or more melodies, each having specific
significance.

Crescendo. Gradually increasing in volume.

Cyclic, Cyclical. A term used loosely to denote any musical
form which has a number of movements such as a sonata,
symphony or suite. More specifically a composition that has

some unifying element, either programmatic or thematic, in each of the movements, e.g., Beethoven's "Pastoral Symphony" and Berlioz' "Symphonie Fantastique."

Development. Unfolding of the thematic materials in a composition by inversion, elaboration, fugal treatment and various combinations of themes, etc.

Diminuendo. Gradually decreasing in volume.

Dynamics. Volume. See (5) page 12.

Elements of Music. The elements of music are: rhythm, melody, harmony, tempo, dynamics, form and color. See page 11.

Ensemble. A group of two or more musicians.

Exoticism. Exoticism in music may be described as musical culture not characteristically European or Western.

Exposition. In a fugue, any section in which the main subject or tune has appeared in all voices or positions. In sonata-allegro form — the section where the main subjects or themes are first presented. See pages 32 and 43.

Expressionism. A radical trend in modern music which started during the second decade of the twentieth century dealing with abstractions — a definite departure from the conventional. The term is a borrowed one. It was first attached to painters such as Picasso, Dali and Klee. See page 94.

Form. The design or structure of a composition. See (6) page 12.

Fugue. A contrapuntal composition with a certain number of voices — usually three or four — written according to certain rules. See page 32.

Gregorian Chant. A monophonic liturgical song in free rhythm used in the Roman Catholic Church. These chants were named after Pope Gregory who was Pope 590–604.

Harmony. Chordal structure or a combination of tones that are sounded simultaneously. See (3) page 11.

Homophonic. Music with a single melody and accompaniment.

Idiom. In music an idiom may be rather loosely defined as being a language or style of composing.

Impressionism. A school of composers in the late nineteenth and early twentieth century (principally Debussy and Ravel who directed their attention and interest toward vagueness and atmosphere in music. See Chapter 9, page 80.

Incidental Music. Music played before or during the action of

136

a play to assist in establishing, supporting or intensifying the mood of the drama. See page 63.

Inversion. A theme is said to be inverted when it is turned upside down.

K. (Köchel). A numbering system by Dr. Ludwig, Ritter von Köchel for cataloging the works of Mozart, e.g., "Jupiter" Symphony K. 551. See Op. (Opus) and L. (Longo).

Key. A family of tones bearing a definite relation to each other.

L. (Longo). A numbering system by Allesandro Longo for cataloging the works of Domenico Scarlatti, e.g., "Cat Fugue" L. 462. Ralph Kirkpatrick has renumbered all the works of Scarlatti and has assigned the letter K. (for Kirkpatrick) 417 to the same work. See K. and Op.

Leitmotif (German spelling: Leitmotiv). Literally this means "leading motif" or a guiding feature in a musical composition or extended work such as an opera. Musical themes or motifs are attached to recurrent ideas, to characters, things, events or states of being in the production. This technique was used extensively by Wagner in his operas. The term "leitmotif" was coined by one of his friends.

Libretto. A text of a long major work such as an opera, oratorio or cantata. Usually the operatic libretto has the original language and a translation into English.

Lied (pl.: lieder). A German Art Song. See Art Song.

Madrigal. In general, an unaccompanied polyphonic song with a secular text. See page 22.

Mass. A commemoration of Christ's sacrifice on the cross. For complete text of the ordinary, see page 23.

Melismatic. Two or more (often many) notes sung to one syllable. The term "melismatic" is used more correctly in connection with the Gregorian chant than any other vocal literature.

Melody. A tune. See (2) page 11.

Mixed Rhythms. Frequent changes of rhythm in one composition.

Monophonic. A single unaccompanied melody.

Motet. In general, an unaccompanied polyphonic song with a sacred text. See page 22.

Motive, Motif (German, Motiv). A fragment of a melody.

Musical Review. Somewhat like an operetta except that very often there is no continuous plot.

<u>Mute</u>. A clasp that is placed on the bridge of a member of the violin family to give it a quiet, sombre and sort of mysterious timbre.

<u>Nationalism</u>. Nationalism in music may be rather loosely defined as music having traits or characteristics of, or influenced by, native folk music, dances and the general culture of the people of a particular country.

<u>Neo-Classicism</u>. A contemporary style of composing which is a return to the eighteenth-century classic point of view as far as clarity, balance of form and transparency of orchestration is concerned. It is a departure from the classic style in that the melodies, harmonies and general presentation are in twentieth-century idioms.

<u>Op. (Opus, Latin)</u>. The abbreviation of the term 'opus' is used in conjunction with figures (Op. 1, Op. 2, etc.) to number the works of a composer. A number is usually assigned to a composition by the composer but in some cases the number is assigned by the publisher. The numbers most often indicate the order in which the compositions were written. Some composers refuse to have their compositions numbered. See *K.* and *L.*

<u>Opera</u>. A drama set to music, either tragic or comic, very often sung throughout. In an operatic production we expect first-rate singing, scenery, costumes, staging and orchestra. Occasionally there is a little spoken dialogue and in some operas the composer and librettist have chosen to include ballet.

<u>Opéra Bouffe (French)</u>. Same as Opéra Comique.

<u>Opera Buffa (Italian)</u>. Same as Opéra Comique.

<u>Opéra Comique (French)</u>. Although there are exceptions, opéra comique is generally an opera with a rather light plot, some spoken dialogue and a happy ending. Comedy often plays an important part and the whole production is more accessible than an opera.

<u>Operetta</u>. A musical comedy with considerable spoken dialogue. The production is not as lavish as an opera. The plot usually appeals to the audience because of its preoccupation with the contemporary scene. Many plots are satirical and have extra-musical implications.

<u>Opus (Op., Latin)</u>. Work. See Op.

<u>Oratorio</u>. A vocal work with an extended libretto which is usually of a religious character. In an oratorio we can expect

138

choruses, solos, duets, etc., with orchestral accompaniment. It is usually designed to be sung without costumes, scenery or action.

Orchestral Tone Color. Tone color of a combination of orchestral instruments. It is usually thought of in connection with a combination of instruments of different timbre.

Ordinary of the Mass. That part of the Mass that remains constant throughout the church calendar or church year.

Overture. There are three different kinds of overtures. They are: 1. Operatic Overture — an orchestral introduction to an opera or similar work, 2. Incidental Overture — an orchestral preface to a play and 3. Concert Overture — an independent concert piece for orchestra. See page 60.

Parallel Motion. Two or more voices in the harmonic or polyphonic structure moving in the same direction keeping the same distance apart.

Percussion. The percussion choir of an orchestra or band is made up of instruments that produce sound when struck, for example, drums, triangle, etc. See page 17.

Pizzicato. A very short note. Plucking the strings of a stringed instrument with the fingers instead of using a bow.

Plainsong. The same as a Gregorian Chant in that it refers to a monophonic liturgical song in free rhythm but in its broadest sense includes the same kind of music of other Christian liturgies such as Anglican and Greek Orthodox as well as non-Christian, e.g., Jewish and Hindu.

Polyphonic. Two or more melodies played or sung simultaneously.

Polyrhythm. The simultaneous use of two different rhythms. See page 97.

Polytonality. Two or more tonalities heard simultaneously. See page 96.

Post-Romantic. The Romantic period is generally confined to the nineteenth century. A few twentieth century composers continue to write in somewhat of a Romantic style. Generally these composers may be called Romanticists or Post-Romanticists. However, the term Post-Romanticism in music applies more specifically to the music of composers who placed even greater emphasis on emotional qualities than their predecessors. These composers also developed greater tone color in orchestration and used more advanced twentieth century harmonic idioms. The approximate dates

139

of Post-Romanticism are from 1890 to 1945. See Chapte
10, page 87.

Program Music. Music in which a composer wishes to portr;
or present some literary or pictorial idea through the
music.

Proper of the Mass. That portion of the Mass which changes
with the church calendar or the liturgical year, such as
Christmas, Easter, etc.

Realism. Musical effects that sound like something real, suc
as wind, storm, etc.

Recapitulation. A restatement of the theme. Sometimes refe
to a repetition of the exposition. See Recapitulation in th
Sonata-Allegro form, pages 42 and 44.

Recitative. For solo voice, usually to be sung in a rather fre
style as far as rhythm and expression are concerned,
placing emphasis on the text. Often syllabic with one no
to a syllable in irregular rhythms becoming rather spee
like. In an opera it is quite often used as a connecting li
between arias, choruses, etc.

Renaissance. A period in art history extending approximatel
from 1400 to 1600. Music of this period is quite predom
nantly polyphonic. See Chapter 4, page 22.

Reprise. Like the term Recapitulation, Reprise has several
meanings depending upon the period of the music in ques
tion. For all practical purposes, to avoid pedantic confu
sion, Recapitulation and Reprise may be thought of as
being synonyms.

Requiem. A mass for the dead.

Review. See Musical Review.

Ripieno. In the Concerto Grosso, the ripieno is the entire o;
chestra. See page 30.

Rhythm. For all practical purposes rhythm is regular recu;
ring accents or beats. See (1) page 11.

Rococo. A period in art history extending approximately fro
1700 to 1775. Rococo music is generally characterized
being graceful and charming with qualities of pleasantne
and elegance. See Chapter 6, page 38.

Romantic. A period in music history generally including the
entire nineteenth century, especially the last seventy-fi
years. Most of the music of the first twenty-five years
definitely Romantic in character but some, especially th
last works of Beethoven (1770-1827) are transitional in

character, having qualities of both the Classic and the
Romantic. See Chapter 8, page 53.

Rondo, Rondo Form, Rondo-Sonata Form. A structural form
in which we have unity created by a recurring theme
(A-B-A-C-A-B-A). There are several kinds of Rondos
but generally speaking it refers to a form somewhat more
extended than the ternary form (A-B-A) and one that has
balance. See bottom of page 45.

Scale. A family of tones having a definite relation to each other
written or played in ascending or descending order. Scales
are generally made up of all or some of the following intervals: half-steps, whole-steps, and step and a half.

Serial Music. Music written with a "tone-row" or a "series"
as a basis. See page 96.

Similar Motion. All voices moving in the same direction but
not necessarily keeping the same distance apart as in
parallel motion.

Singspiel (German). The ancestor of German Romantic Opera.
The German equivalent of Opéra comique. See Opéra
Comique.

Sonata. The term was first used during the Renaissance period.
It was then used very loosely to indicate any instrumental
music in contrast to vocal music which was for the most
part referred to as "cantata" or music to be sung. Generally, from the Classic period on, the term "sonata"
refers to an instrumental solo, e.g., for piano, for violin,
etc. In its broadest sense the term is used to denote a
structural form. For details of the classic sonata see
"The Symphony a Sonata" pages 41 to 47.

Sonata-Allegro Form, Sonata-Form. These two terms are
identical. The structural form used in the first movement
of a typical classic sonata. In this book the term "Sonata-
Allegro Form" is used to avoid confusion between Sonata-
Form and the Sonata. For detailed discussion see page 43.

Song Cycle. A series of art songs having some psychological
association with each other, the same general character
or some general unifying element that makes the entire
collection an entity.

Staccato. A very short note.

Syllabic. In any vocal work where there is one note to a syllable.

Symphonic Tone Poem. An orchestral composition in free form,
designed by the composer to present certain literary or

pictorial ideas. The form of the composition is usually determined by the pictorial or literary content.

Symphony. A sonata for symphony orchestra. See page 41.

Tempo. The speed at which a composition is performed. See (4) page 12.

Ternary Form. A form made up of two sections, the first cal "A" and the second called "B." The pattern of the ternar form is generally A-B-A but is quite often A-A-B-A.

Theme. A melody or musical idea. The same as the subject used in a fugue or a sonata. See pages 32 and 43.

Timbre. The quality of color of the sound of an individual in strument or human voice, e.g., various instruments and voices, when sounding the same pitch, have different ton qualities.

Tone. A sound that has regular vibrations giving it a definite pitch.

Tone Color. The psychological association of sound and colc See glossary definitions of "color" and "timbre."

Tone-Row. All of the twelve pitches within the octave, arranged in some arbitrary sequence and used as the basi and source of material for an entire composition. The tone-row is also known as "series." See page 96.

Transparency of Orchestration. Orchestral music in which the listener can quite readily distinguish each and all in strument(s) or family(ies) of instruments is said to have transparency.

Trio. A composition for three voices or three instruments. The term is sometimes used to designate the middle sec tion of a ternary form. See page 46.

Tutti. In the Concerto Grosso the tutti is the entire orchestr See page 30.

Twelve-Tone Technique. A method of writing music, using a twelve chromatic pitches in a "tone-row." See page 95.

Variations. A theme is first presented in a rather straightforward manner. It is then modified and embellished in any number of ways. These are called variations. All variations retain the essential features and have sometl in common with the theme. Sometimes the association tween theme and variation is rather obvious while in an other variation this association may be quite obscure.

Whole-Tone Scale. A scale made up of whole-steps, six equ intervals to the octave.

Italian Terms for Speeds

The following is a list of some of the most commonly used Italian terms which indicate tempi or speeds of various movements of the sonata or other compositions. This listing is from slow to fast.

Grave — the slowest tempo in music

Largo — very slow

Adagio or Lento — slow, a little faster than Largo

Andante — fairly slow

Andantino — a little faster than andante

Moderato — moderately fast

Allegretto — fairly fast

Allegro — fast

Vivace — lively, faster than allegro

Presto — very fast

Prestissimo — as fast as possible

There are other terms modifying these tempo terms such as:

Allegro assai — very fast

Allegro non troppo — fast but not too fast

Allegro con brio — fast with fire

Allegro moderato — fast with moderation

Tempo di menuetto — speed of a minuet

Andante cantabile — fairly slow in a singing style

Andante tranquillo — fairly slow and tranquil

Andante con moto — fairly slow with motion

etc., etc.

These terms as well as the notation and other indications for interpretation are universal. All music may be played and is understood by musicians all over the world.

Suggested Reading

American Music
    America's Music, Gilbert Chase —
        McGraw-Hill, New York.
    Modern Music Makers, Madelein Gross —
        E. P. Dutton and Co., New York.

Appreciation
    An Introduction to Music, Martin Bernstein —
        Prentice-Hall, Inc., New York.
    An Introduction to Music, David D. Boyden —
        Alfred A. Knopf, New York.
    The Enjoyment of Music, Joseph Machlis —
        W. W. Norton, New York.

Bells
    Bells of All Nations, Ernest Morris —
        Robert Hall, Limited, London.
    The Carillon, Frank Percival Price —
        Oxford University Press, London.

Biographies
    American Composers Today, David Ewen —
        H. W. Wilson Co., New York.
    Composers of Yesterday, David Ewen —
        H. W. Wilson Co., New York.
    European Composers Today, David Ewen —
        H. W. Wilson Co., New York.

(These three books contain biographies and short discussions of the composers' music and lists of principal works.)

Chamber Music
    Chamber Music, Homer Ulrich —
        Columbia University Press, New York.

Composers' letters and writings about music
    Composers on Music, Sam Morgenstern —
        Pantheon Books Inc., New York.

Dictionary
    Harvard Dictionary of Music, Willi Apel —
        Harvard University Press, Cambridge, Mass.

Encyclopedia of Music
    Groves Dictionary —
        St. Martin's Press, New York.

Form in Music
    Foundations of Music, Wayne Barlow —
        Appleton-Century-Crofts, New York.
    The Structure of Music, Robert Erickson —
        Noonday Press, New York.
    What to Listen for in Music, Aaron Copland —
        McGraw-Hill, New York.

History of Music
    A History of Western Music, Donald Jay Grout —
        W. W. Norton, New York.

Instruments of the Orchestra
    The History of Musical Instruments, Curt Sachs —
        W. W. Norton, New York.
    The Story of Musical Instruments, H. W. Schwartz —
        Doubleday, Garden City, N. J.

Jazz
    Hear Me Talkin' to Ya, Nat Shapiro and Nat Hentoff —
        Holt, Rinehart & Winston, New York.

Opera
    Operas and Musical Comedies, J. Walker McSpadden —
        Thomas Y. Crowell Co., New York.
    A Short History of Opera, Donald Jay Grout —
        Columbia University Press, New York.

Organ
    The Contemporary American Organ, William Harrison
        Barnes — J. Fischer and Bros., New York.

Piano
> Literature of the Piano, Ernest Hutcheson —
> > Alfred A. Knopf, New York.

Program Notes
> Analytical Concert Guide, Louis Biancolli —
> > Doubleday, Garden City, N. J.
> Masterworks of the Orchestral Repertoire, Donald N.
> > Ferguson — University of Minnesota Press,
> > Minneapolis, Minn.

Pronunciation
> NBC Handbook of Pronunciation, James F. Bender —
> > Thomas Y. Crowell Company, New York.

Recorded Music
> Guide to Long-Playing Records —
> > Alfred A. Knopf, New York.
> > Vol. 1. Orchestral Music, Irving Kolodin.
> > Vol. 2. Vocal Music, Philip L. Miller.
> > Vol. 3. Chamber and Solo Instrument Music,
> > > Harold C. Schönberg.
> How to Build a Record Library, Howard Taubman —
> > Hanover House, New York.
> The High Fidelity Magazine, The Magazine for Music
> > Listeners, The Publishing House, Great Barrington,
> > Mass.

Symphony Orchestra and Symphonic Music
> The American Symphony Orchestra, John H. Mueller —
> > Indiana University Press, Bloomington, Indiana.
> Symphonic Music, Homer Ulrich —
> > Columbia University Press, New York.

Twentieth-Century Music
> Introduction to Contemporary Music, Joseph Machlis —
> > W. W. Norton, New York.
> Music Since 1900, Nicolas Slonimsky —
> > Coleman-Ross Co., New York.

Indexes

158

INDEX OF LISTENING TECHNIQUES

This includes not only listening techniques but in some cases what to expect of the music, how to prepare yourself for listening, what to listen for and your responsibility as a listener. For further information see Index of Forms, Types and Medium.

Name_____Section_____

MY RECORD LIBRARY

_____

_____

_____

_____

_____

_____

_____

_____

_____

_____

_____

_____

_____

_____

_____

_____

_____

_____

_____

_____

_____

Name_____Section_____

MY RECORD LIBRARY

_____

_____

_____

_____

_____

_____

_____

_____

_____

_____

_____

_____

_____

_____

_____

_____

_____

_____

_____

_____

_____

WORK SHEET NO. 1

Check the instruments that you hear.

		1	2	3	4	5	6	7	8	9	10	11	12
STRING	Violin												
	Viola												
	'Cello												
	Double Bass												
	Harp												
	Harpsichord												
	Piano												
WOOD WIND	Piccolo												
	Flute												
	Clarinet												
	Saxophone												
	Oboe												
	English Horn												
	Bassoon												
BRASS	Trumpet												
	French Horn												
	Trombone												
	Tuba												
PERCUSSION	Kettle-Drum												
	Bass Drum												
	Snare Drum												
	Cymbals												
	Triangle												
	Xylophone												
	Celesta												
	Other												

WORK SHEET NO. 2

Andante con moto, Symphony No. 5 Beethoven

Check the choirs that play part or all of the following:	String Choir	Wood-Wind Choir	Brass Choir
I - Theme_____ 1			
Echo passage_____ 2			
II - 1st period - Theme_____ 3			
II - 2nd period - Theme_____ 4			
I - Variation No. 1_____ 5			
II - 1st period - Variation No. 1_____ 6			
II - 2nd period - Variation No. 1_____ 7			
I - Variation No. 2_____ 8			
I - Variation No. 3_____ 9			
I - Variation No. 4_____ 10			
Subordinate Theme - (after very soft repeated chords in strings) 11			
II - 2nd period - Theme_____ 12			
Returning passage - Retransition _____ 13			
I - Theme_____ 14			
Coda _____ 15			

Name_____ Section _____

Name of band or orchestra _____

WORK SHEET NO. 3

Sketch in a seating plan of some particular band or orchestra. Do not copy conventional plan given in this book.

Name_____ Section _____

WORK SHEET NO. 4

Check any of these expressive qualities that you hear in the music.	Composition	1	2	3	4	5	6
Amorous_____							
Brilliant_____							
Calm_____							
Charming_____							
Delicate_____							
Devotional_____							
Doleful_____							
Dramatic_____							
Festive_____							
Gay_____							
Gloomy_____							
Glorious_____							
Graceful_____							
Heroic_____							
Joyous_____							
Majestic_____							
Melancholy_____							
Mysterious_____							
Noisy_____							
Pleasant_____							
Sad_____							
Serious_____							
Singable_____							
Sinister_____							
Thrilling_____							
Turbulent_____							
Vigorous_____							
Other							
_____							
_____							

WORK SHEET NO. 5

Check the qualities or characteristics that you hear.

	1	2	3	4	5	6	7	8
RHYTHM								
Easy to follow								
Difficult to follow								
MELODY								
Clear, distinct								
Songlike								
Vague								
Unpredictable								
Obscure								
EMOTION								
Supressed								
Restrained								
Unrestrained								
Emphasized								
TONE COLORS								
Colorless								
Transparent								
Colorful								
Atmospheric								
QUALITIES OF								
Renaissance								
Baroque								
Rococo								
Classic								
Romantic								
Impressionistic								
Expressionistic								
Neo-Classic								
Post-Romantic								
Popular								
MEDIUM OR FORM (Write in) (Examples: string quartet, vocal solo, organ solo, orchestra, piano concerto, etc.)								
	1	2	3	4	5	6	7	8

Questionnaire

Name_____Section_____Date____
     (Please print last name first)

Home town and state_____

Year in School_____Major_____

HOME ENVIRONMENT (Check only when the answer is "yes.")

1. Are either of your parents interested in music?   Enthusiastic?
2. Does your home have TV?   Radio? Record player (LP)?
3. Does your family have an LP "Classical" library?   Jazz?   Popular?
4. Has your family attended any of the following? If more than once double-check. Artist concert series?   Opera?   Symphony? Ballet?   Musical comedy?   Jazz concert?   String quartet concert?   Soloist (instrumental or vocal)?

YOUR LISTENING EXPERIENCE (Check only when answer is "yes.")

1. Have you attended a concert by a major symphony orchestra?   Soloist?   String quartet?   Opera?   Operetta?   Band? Big name Jazz band?   Musical comedy? An artist concert series?
2. Do you arrange your work so that you may be able to attend concerts and musical events on the campus?
3. How many concerts have you heard during the past year?
4. Check the kind of music you like best (one or more). Symphony   Band   Opera Operetta   Ballet   Concertos Organ   Piano   Violin   Vocal solos   Vocal groups   String Quartet Jazz

Questionnaire (Cont.)

5. Have you a "classical" record collection?
   Popular?   Jazz?
6. Do you expect to start a "classical" record collection?   Jazz?   Popular?
7. Do you listen to recorded music with friends?
   Often?   Occasionally?
8. Do you discuss the music with your friends before
   playing?   During the playing?
   After?
9. Have you ever followed the score of any music
   while listening to it?
10. Do you own: Music Dictionary?   History of
    music?   . Another book on music apprecia-
    tion?   Biography of any composer?
    Any other book about music?
11. Have you read a book about music during the past

    year?   Name it.
12. Are you a subscriber to a music magazine?

    Name it.

YOUR PARTICIPATION EXPERIENCE (Check only when
    answer is "yes.")

1. Do you play a musical instrument?

   Name it.   Sing?
2. Have you played in a high school orchestra?
   Band?   Years experience?
3. Have you sung in a high school choral organization?   Years?
4. Are you playing or singing in the college orchestra?   Band?   Organized vocal group?
   Church choir?
5. During the past year have you sung a solo?
   Played an instrumental solo?